A Celebration of the Household

A Celebration of the Household

The Classic Guide to Running Your Home

By L. G. Abell

SKYHORSE PUBLISHING

Skyhorse Publishing books may be purchased in bulk at special discounts for sales promotion, corporate gifts, fund-raising, or educational purposes. Special editions can also be created to specifications. For details, contact the Special Sales Department, Skyhorse Publishing, 307 West 36th Street, 11th Floor, New York, NY 10018 or info@skyhorsepublishing.com.

Skyhorse® and Skyhorse Publishing® are registered trademarks of Skyhorse Publishing, Inc. ®, a Delaware corporation.

www.skyhorsepublishing.com

10 9 8 7 6 5 4 3 2 1

ISBN: 978-1-62087-714-2

Library of Congress Cataloging-in-Publication Data is available on file.

Printed in India

Table of Contents

PUBLISHER'S PREFACE

This work is the production of a highly gifted and disciplined mind. In it the authoress gives us the result of fifteen years of careful and extended observation, while acting in the twofold character of a Christian mother, and an experienced and practical housewife. It is in truth, as will be seen at a glance, a treasury of useful knowledge and sound practical wisdom; a store-house of principles and facts, embodying more useful information on the various topics on which it treats than any similar work with which we are acquainted. Its object is twofold, viz: to promote the temporal comfort and spiritual interests of families. This object, it aims to accomplish by teaching, in the broadest sense, the science of life. Though not written in the form of a regular treatise, the subject is presented in three aspects, moral, physical, and economical. *Moral*, which relates to the religious education and government of children; *physical*, which relates to the condition, infirmities, wants, and management of infants; *economical*, or the art of living, of promoting and preserving health, and in general the right disposition and regulation of household affairs in conformity with the dictates of prudence and sound discretion.

In these several points of view, the subject is invested with peculiar interest to parents and heads of families. To those whose special duty it is to preside over domestic concerns, the great amount of information given in so narrow a compass relative to the healing and culinary arts is invaluable. To make it both a safe and useful family directory, the ablest medical treatises, and the most approved works on cookery, have been diligently consulted and compared. While, then, the work unfolds and enforces the principles of sound Christian morality, it embodies all that is necessary for ordinary purposes in a treatise on domestic medicine, and the most important and valuable secrets of the culinary art.

The authoress, with a sort of careless ease, notes down her observations and gives only such plain and cogent instructions as sink into the mind by their own weight. Nevertheless, the work bears the impress of a strong and vigorous mind, if not the stamp of marked originality, and is replete with valuable hints, sparkling thoughts, and just sentiments. It is a fact that the most splendid exhibitions of genius are not always the most useful. Those writings, which like Bacon's Essays, "come home to the business and bosoms of men," are destined to produce the most beneficial influence, if not to endure the longest. A work adapted to the common purposes of life is of more real value than more pompous and erudite volumes. An honest and benevolent mind will be satisfied with being in some measure useful, without aspiring to great conspicuity. Such an one will be less anxious to accumulate praise, than to discharge the humble duty assigned to him by providence. If our authoress has supplied the public with a valuable household directory, in all the great duties and concerns of domestic life, she has not written in vain, nor will she lose her reward.

The Publisher

Chapter 1: MISCELLANEOUS MORAL HINTS ON THE FORMATION OF CHARACTER, HABITS, ETC.

EXCELLENCE THE REWARD OF INDUSTRY

Excellence is providentially placed beyond the reach of indolence, that success may be the reward of industry, and that idleness may be punished with obscurity and disgrace.

TRAINING OF THE MIND

A sound moral discipline and a well regulated mind can, under God, carry a man through life so that he will not be the sport and victim of every change that flits across the scene. And it cannot be too anxiously borne in mind, that this great attainment is in a remarkable degree under the influence of habit.

Every day that passes, and every step that we take, without making it the object of earnest attention, renders the acquirement more difficult and uncertain, until a period at length arrives when no power exists in the mind capable of correcting the disorder that habit has fixed. The frivolous mind may then continue frivolous to the last, amusing itself with trifles, or creating for itself fictions of the fancy, no better than dreams. The distorted mind may continue to the last eagerly pursuing its speculations, departing for her from the truth; and the vitiated mind may continue to the last, the slave of its impure and degrading passions. Such is the power, and such the result of mental habits. We cannot determine how many acts of frivolity may constitute the permanently frivolous mind; how many trains of impure thought may constitute the corrupted mind; or what degrees of inattention to the diligent culture of the powers within may be fatal to our best interests. In early life, aim at the mastery of the mind; give earnest attention to the trains of thought encouraged, as habits may be thus unconsciously formed, the influence of which may be permanent and irremediable, and peril the happiness of life and the immortal interests of the soul.

RESOLUTION

There is nothing in man so potential for weal or woe as firmness of purpose. Resolution is almost omnipotent. Sheridan was at first timid, and was obliged to sit down in the midst of a speech. Confounded, and mortified at the cause of his failure, he said one day to a friend, "It is in me, and it shall come out." From that moment, he rose, and shone, and triumphed in consummate eloquence. Here was true moral courage. It was well observed by a heathen moralist, that it is not because things are difficult that we dare not undertake them. Be then bold in spirit. Indulge no doubts, for doubts are traitors. In the practical pursuit of our high aim, let us not lose sight of it in the slightest instance; for it is more by a disregard of small things, than by open and flagrant offences, that men come short of excellence. There is always a right and a wrong, and if you ever doubt, be sure you take not the wrong. Observe this rule, and every experience will be to you a means of advancement.

PUNCTUALITY

Method is the very hinge of business; and there is no method without punctuality. A want of this virtue would throw the whole world into a state of confusion and disorder. Punctuality is important, because it is not only the golden chain of the universe, but it also promotes the peace, order, good temper, and happiness of a family. The want of it not only infringes on necessary duty, but sometimes excludes it. The calmness of mind that it produces is another advantage of punctuality. A disorderly person is always in a hurry, and has no time. Punctuality gives weight to character, and like other virtues, it propagates itself. Servants and children will be punctual where their leader is so.

PATIENCE

As the bee extracts sweets from the bitterest plants, so the patient and resigned spirit derives instruction and even happiness from the severest misfortunes and the sorest trials.

FORGIVENESS

A more glorious victory cannot be gained over another than this: when the injury began on his part, the kindness begins on ours.

TALENTS

Dig them up—bring them to the light—turn them over, polish them, and they will give light to the world. You know not what you are capable of doing; you cannot sound the ocean of thought within you. You must labor, keep at it, and dig deep and long before you will begin to realize much. Be inactive—mourn because you were not created a giant in intellect—and you will die a fool.

THE YOUTHFUL MIND

A straw will make an impression on the virgin snow, but after a time a horse's hoof cannot penetrate it; so it is with the youthful mind. A trifling word may make an impression, but after a few years the most powerful appeals may cease to influence it.

Think of this ye who have the training of the infant mind, and leave such impressions thereon as will be safe to carry amid the follies and temptations of the world.

TIME

God, who is liberal in all other gifts, shows us, by his own wise economy, how circumspect we should be in the management of our time, for he never gives us two moments together. He only gives us the second when he takes away the first, and keeps the third in his own hands, leaving us in absolute uncertainty whether it shall ever become ours or not!

REPROOF

Never reprove anyone when they are angry. But go in the cool of reason, and passion, when all is quiet within, for then you have the greatest probability of success.

LITTLE THINGS NO TRIFLES

The nerve of a tooth, not as large as the finest cambric needle, will sometimes drive a strong man to distraction. A musquetoe can make an elephant absolutely mad. The coral rock, which causes a navy to founder, is the work of an insect. The warrior that withstood death in a thousand forms may be killed by an insect. The deepest wretchedness often results from a perpetual continuation of petty trials. The formation of character often depends on circumstances apparently the most trivial; an impulse, a casual conversation, a chance visit, or something equally unimportant has changed the whole destiny of life, and has resulted in virtue or vice—in weal or in woe !

HOW TO MAKE HOME HAPPY

It is not the imposing majesty of a sumptuous mansion, nor the hollow glare of gaudy furniture, nor the obsequious attention of servants, that make the blessedness of home. No, it is the steady exercise of those holy charities that soothes our sorrows, and that builds the nest of peace, love, and true enjoyment in our bosoms. It is mutual respect and attention, a kind consideration of each other's feelings, under all circumstances—a sympathy in our cares, a regard to our interests, the exercise of a patient, forbearing, and forgiving temper, that makes home the "only Paradise that has survived the fall." And let it never be forgotten that even a smile or a frown may gild

with brightness, or overcast with clouds, the whole horizon of that sacred spot—*home.*

AN UNSUBDUED TEMPER

Beware of that being, who indulges in an uncontroled temper, if you desire peace and happiness. Many a lofty mind and noble genius has by its influence become the bane of friendship, the curse of home, and the dread of society. It destroys the peace of families, poisons the fountains of happiness, and dries up the source of every pleasure. Beauty, wit, wealth, talents, fame, and honor can never be a substitute. This one gem outweighs them all: an *ambiable temper.*

THE VALUE OF TIME

"I shall only be idle a minute." A minute! in this time many a noble action has been performed. A minute! when resolutions have been made that have changed the after current of life. A minute! in the space which a tear reached the eye of the repentant prodigal.

NEGLIGENCE

There is a carelessness about some young persons that is manifest in almost everything they do. Regardless of the future, or the opinions of others, they rush forward in some new project, and before they see their error, it is impossible to retrace their steps. If they attempt to study, it is done superficially. If they work, it is often performed unfaithfully. When anything new is presented to their minds, they enter into it with all

their hearts, to the neglect of what may be of greater importance, and by frequently changing their plans and pursuits, they fail to succeed. Minds capable of high efforts—of splendid achievements, of extensive usefulness—have been paralyzed by its influence.

DISCONTENT

A man of discontented mind and ungovernable passions can scarcely find a situation where he will be happy. Give him wealth, honor, luxury, ease, and all the comfort that earth can afford, still his own irritable spirit, superinduced by his own lack of moral and mental culture, will poison all.

TRUTH

The heaviest fetter that ever weighed down the limbs of a captive is as the web of the gossamer compared with the pledge of a man of honor. The wall of stone and the bar of iron may be broken, but his plighted word *never*.

SCANDAL

Those who possess the least inherent purity are the most apt to traduce and vilify others. The slanderer judges after the dictates of his own malicious heart, and thus impugns the actions, motives, and feelings of others.

KINDNESS

Help others and you relieve yourself. Go out and drive away the cloud from that friend's brow, and you will return with a lighter heart. A word may blight the brightest hope; a word may revive the dying. A frown may crush a gentle heart. The smile of love or forgiveness may relieve from torture.

GRATITUDE

Be careful to teach your children gratitude. Lead them to acknowledge every favor that they receive; to speak often of their benefactors, and to ask blessings for them. Accustom them to treat with marked attention their instructors and those who have aided them in the attainment of knowledge or piety. Gratitude is one of our first duties to God, and should not be forgotten when due to man.

TEMPER

No trait of character is more valuable than the possession of a good temper. Home can never be made happy without it. It is like flowers that spring up in our pathway, reviving and cheering us. Kind words and looks are the outward demonstrations; patience and forbearance are the sentinels within. Study to acquire and retain a sweet temper. It is more valuable than

gold—it captivates more than beauty, and to the close of life retains its freshness and power.

POLITENESS

Good breeding is both sanctioned and suggested by enlightened reason. Its principles are founded in a love of virtue and a just appreciation of the rights of others. It is by discipline and effort that we attain to that elevation of character that enables and inclines us to practice self-denial and consult the honor and happiness of others. Let no one think it of little consequence whether he has the manners of a clown or a gentleman. Politeness is a passport to the respect and friendship of the refined and intelligent, and wins favor even from the vulgar. It is benevolence and kindness carried into the details of life, and throws a charm around its most common scenes. Let it be cultivated, and its beauties will daily unfold; with time and patience the leaf of the mulberry tree becomes satin.

MILDNESS

Be always as mild as you can; honey attracts more flies than vinegar. If you err let it be on the side of gentleness. The human mind is so constituted that it resists severity and yields to softness.

SPARE MINUTES

Spare minutes are the gold dust of time. Of all the portions of our life, spare moments are or may be the most fruitful of evil. They are gaps through which temptations find the easiest access to our hearts. Let them all be improved with care; "Sands make the mountains as moments make years."

THE ORDER OF A HOUSEHOLD

To establish order in the household, one of the first things necessary is to adopt rules for its internal arrangement and government. Let there be a fixed time for meals, for worship, and for retirement. Let punctuality be required from each member, and soon the habit will become fixed and permanent. This greatly helps to give stability and symmetry to the character, and will save from many a snare.

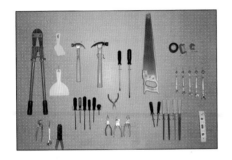

INDUSTRY AND ENERGY

Resolution, energy, spirit, and courage, with a faithful improvement of time, will attain any position and overcome any obstacle. An ordinary intellect will, by industry and perseverance, often accomplish more than a much superior one, deficient in energy and the power of endurance.

CHEERFULNESS

Those who benefit the world by their labors, who here remove a weed and there plant a flower, must be cheerful. Amidst the most adverse circumstances there are still reasons for cheerfulness. So long as there are motives to gratitude, there is cause for cheerfulness.

GIVE A FEW MINUTES TO THAT CHILD

Few parents realize how much their children may be taught at home, by devoting a few minutes to their instruction every day. Let the parent make the experiment only during the hours that are not spent in school. Let him make a companion of his child, converse with him, propose questions, answer inquiries, communicate facts, and explain difficulties, the meaning of things, and the reason of things, and all in so easy and agreeable manner that it will be no task, but it will serve to awaken curiosity and interest the mind, and he will be astonished at the progress he will make.

SCOLDING

I never knew one who was in the habit of scolding able to govern a family. What makes people scold? The want of self-government. How then can they govern others! Those who govern well are generally calm. They are prompt and resolute, but steady and mild.

TO ACQUIRE A GOOD REPUTATION

Endeavor to *be*, rather than to *appear* good. Seize the present opportunity, and improve it to the utmost in doing your duty. Be more ready to commend than blame. If you have occasion to reprove, first convince by actual kindness that it is your design to do the person good. Be faithful in everything however small. Be honest in all your dealings, and always do to others as you would be done by. Let all know that you value your honor, and this may induce them to value their own.

PARENTAL COMMANDS

If you wish to be obeyed, be careful to make few commands, and see that they are obeyed. Run no hazard in giving orders that may by any possibility be disobeyed. If you make them, let nothing be an excuse for disobedience.

WHAT EDUCATION SHOULD BE

The foundation of education should be laid in the knowledge and love of God. Education, without moral training, is like a sword in the hands of a madman. "Knowledge is power" for good or for evil. See to it then that your children are trained in the principles of religion, honesty, integrity and virtue, obedience, self-government, benevolence, and kindness. They need line upon line, precept upon precept, and constant watchfulness over faults and habits. No schools however well conducted, no colleges however high in literary advantages, without this care and effort to establish correct principles and to form the character to virtue can be safe for your children. They should be taught moreover, that they must be, under the blessing of God, the manufacturers of their own fortunes. Many parents toil and labour, and deny themselves the comforts of life to hoard up wealth for their children. But fit them to take care of themselves, and it will be of more value than the wealth of the Indies. The earlier you teach them to depend upon their own resources the better. See that their morals are pure, their minds are cultivated, and their whole natures are subservient to the laws of God, and it will be of greater value than the riches of the world. Train them up to habits of industry, economy, and virtue, and it will be the best estate they can have, of which no misfortune can deprive them.

THE INFLUENCE OF THE ELDEST CHILD

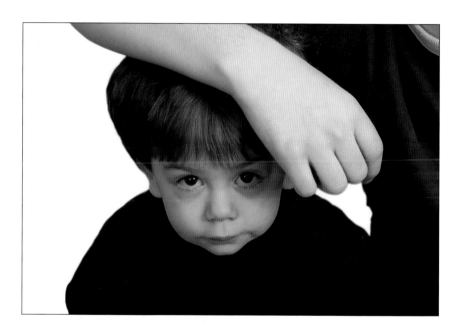

The eldest child will be a model after which the younger members of the family will be fashioned. The taste, the habits, the character of the one, will very likely be copied by the others. How great the responsibility of the parent in the culture and training then of the eldest child!

SLEEP

A proper degree of exercise is necessary both for body and mind. When nature calls for rest, obey her dictates. In good health seven or eight hours sleep is generally sufficient. In sickness sleep is often more valuable than medicine in restoring the exhausted powers and deranged functions, and when the patient can sleep it is like the "balm of Gilead" to the debilitated frame.

IMPROVEMENT OF TIME

Do small things, as writing a letter, making a sketch, reading a review, etc., in your leisure moments; leaving the body of the day to more important affairs. Instead of saying much about your employments or wasting time in procrastination and dread of them, set yourself quietly, promptly, resolutely about your work, and you may save hours for the acquisition of some important art or science. Always have convenient work at hand, that your time may be usefully employed during a social call or in moments of

leisure. Much time and labor will be saved by always keeping things in order. Devise methods of expediting labor, and give to each branch its due importance. There is time enough for every work and duty; if anything is neglected from a supposed want of time the fault is ours.

FRANKLIN'S CODE OF MORALS

Eat not to fullness—drink not to elevation—speak not but what may benefit others or yourself—avoid trifling conversation. Let everything have its place, let each part of your business have its time. Resolve to perform what you ought—perform without fail what you resolve. Make no expense but to do good to others or yourself, wasting nothing. Lose no time, be always employed in something useful. Use no deceit, think innocently and justly, and if you speak, speak accordingly. Wrong none by injuries, or omitting the benefits which are your duty. Avoid extremes, forbear resenting injuries. Suffer no uncleanliness in your body, clothes, or habitation. Be not disturbed about trifles, or at accidents common or unavoidable. Imitate Jesus Christ.

Chapter 2: PARENTS

PRACTICAL THOUGHTS

Be yourselves what your children should be. Avoid what they should avoid at all times; let your example be a safe and unerring guide. Are there defects in their character? Inquire the cause, whether it may not be owing to some defect or fault in your own character which they have copied.

MAXIMS FOR PARENTS AND TEACHERS

Never give reproof if it can be avoided while the feelings of either party are excited. If the parent or teacher be not calm, his influence is diminished, and a bad example is set. If the child is much excited or provoked, he will not feel the force of argument or rebuke. On the other hand, do not defer too long. Seize the first favorable opportunity while the circumstances are fresh in memory. Reprove each fault as it occurs, and not suffer them to accumulate lest the offender be discouraged by the amount. Let your reproofs be frequent enough to convince the child that he is observed, but not so frequent as to tire. Never expose a fault to others, unless as a last resort. It blunts a child's sensibility, it discourages effort, it diminishes confidence in the reprover, and it excites a feeling of triumph in associates and of envy in the offender, rather than a just sense of the fault.

HINTS FOR PARENTS

Never allow a child to be uncourteous and disrespectful, in language or behaviour, to yourself or others. Cultivate the affections with greater care than you would nurse a house plant; they afford more pleasure in the domestic circle, and their frailty demands your utmost attention. Allow no influences in your family but those that are gentle and kind. Teach your children to respect age and never allow them to speak lightly of religious or serious things. Never be absent yourselves from church, nor suffer your child to be, unless for some cause that would prevent weekday occupations or pleasures. Keep your children employed, and they will have less time to contract bad habits; know where they are, and what they are doing, that you may guard them from danger.

RELIGIOUS EDUCATION

There is not a blessing of our life, not a joy of our hearts, not a pure emotion within our bosoms, or a ray of hope shed upon our pathway, that has not had its origin in religion, and may be traced in all its hallowed, healthful influences to the Bible. With the dawn of childhood then, in the earliest days of intelligence, should the mind be impressed and stored with religious truth, and nothing should be allowed to exclude or efface it. It should be taught so early that the mind will never remember when it began to learn; it will then have the character of innate, inbred principles incorporated with their very being.

PARENTAL EXAMPLE

Never forget that the first book children read is their parent's example, their daily deportment. If this is forgotten, you may find in the loss of your domestic peace that your children only know the right path, but still follow the wrong.

OBEDIENCE

Remember, if you would not have all your instructions and councils ineffectual, teach your children to obey. Government in a family is the great safeguard of religion and morals, the support of order, and the source of prosperity. Nothing has a greater tendency to bring a curse upon a family than the insubordination and disobedience of children, and there is no more painful and disgusting sight than on ungoverned child.

BEAUTIFUL, YET FEARFUL THOUGHT

Childhood is like a mirror catching and reflecting images all around it. Remember that an impious, profane, or vulgar thought may operate upon a young heart, like a careless spray of water thrown upon polished steel, staining it with rust that no after efforts can efface.

NURSERY MAXIMS

Remember that children are men and women in miniature, and though they should be allowed to act as children, still our dealings with them should be manly, and not morose; recollect, also, that every look, word, tone, and gesture, nay even your dress, makes an impression.

Never correct a child on suspicion, or without understanding the whole matter, nor trifle with a child's feelings when under discipline.

Be always mild and cheerful in their presence, communicative but never extravagant, trifling, or vulgar in language or gesture. Never trifle with a child, nor speak beseechingly, when it is doing wrong. Always follow commands with a close and careful watch, until the thing is done, allowing no evasion, and no modification, unless the child ask for it, and it be expressly granted.

Never reprove children severely in company, nor hold them up to ridicule, or make light of their failings.

Never speak in an impatient, fretful manner, if you have occasion to find fault.

Never say to a child, "I do not believe what you say," nor even express doubts. If you have such feelings, keep them to yourself, and wait; truth will eventually be made plain.

Never disappoint the confidence a child reposes in you, whether it be a thing placed in your care or a promise.

Always give prompt attention to a child when he speaks, so as to prevent repeated calls, and that he may learn to give prompt attention when you call him.

At the table a child should be taught to sit up and behave in a becoming manner, not to tease when denied, or to leave his chair without asking. A parent's wish at such a time should be a law, from which no appeal should be made.

Even in sickness, gentle restraint is better for the child than indulgence.

Never try to impress a child with religious truth when in anger, or talk to him of God, as it will not have the desired effect. Do it under more favorable circumstances.

Improve the first ten years of life as the golden opportunity, which may never return. It is the seed time, and your harvest depends upon the seed then sown.

There should never be two sets of manners, the one for home and the other for company, but a gentle behavior should be always required.

Selfishness that binds the miser in chains, that chills the heart, must never be allowed a place in the family circle. Teach the child to share his gifts and pleasures with others, to be obliging, kind, and benevolent, and the influence of such instruction may come back into your own bosom to bless your latest hour.

Dread an insubordinate temper. Deal with it as one of the greatest of evils. Let the child feel by your manner, that he is not a safe companion for the rest of the family when in anger. Allow no one to speak to him at such times, not even to answer a question; take from him books, and whatever he may have, and place him where he shall feel that the indulgence of a bad temper shall deprive him of all enjoyment, and he will soon learn to control it himself.

GENERAL RULES OF CONDUCT, AND DEMEANOR

Propriety of deportment is a happy union of the moral and the graceful, and should be considered in two points of view; and it ought, therefore, to direct us in our important duties, as well as in our more trifling enjoyments. It is the result of a knowledge of oneself and of respect for the rights of others. The usages of the world are often the imitations of propriety, and if not based on sincerity become inconstant in everything. It is this false politeness, this superficial observance of the mere form, that leads people to be suspicious of that which is genuine. Truth, benevolence, and kindness are the soul of genuine politeness; it is both the effect and cause of Christian civilization, and always attends upon the effort to do what is right. It is so important to every individual, that neither rank, talents, fortune, nor beauty can dispense with it, nor can anything inspire affection like its winning charms. "Manners" says one, "are more important than laws." These touch us but here and there, now and then, but *manners* are what vex or soothe us, corrupt or purify, exalt or debase, barbarize or refine, by a constant, steady, uniform, insensible operation, like the air we breathe in. They give the whole form and color to our lives; according to their quality, they *aid* morals or *destroy* them.

To avoid wounding the feelings of others is the key to the secret; and he who will always regulate his sayings and doings by that principle will rarely violate any of the essentials of good breeding. Judgment and attention are necessary to fulfill this precept, for by inadvertance or indiscretion, as much pain may be given as by designed malevolence.

Civilities always merit acknowledgment. If you have been received with respect and kindness when away from home, you owe it to those who have entertained you to inform them of your safe return, and to thank them for their kindness and hospitality. Accommodate yourself to every grade of persons and every class of society; but never sacrifice principles. Abhor everything profane, licentious, intemperate and vulgar. The only way to deal with the courteous is to be courteous; it is the best way, also, to deal with the rude. Contempt and haughtiness are never wise and never politic. It is plain at a glance that arrogance and incivility are never the test of good breeding; they are utterly inconsistent with true dignity. A man's pride should only dwell in his *principles*, and not in his demeanor; he should be above everything which may be unworthy of his nature, and above doing anything which shall lessen his dignity or impair his honor. Civility teaches us to treat with proportionate respect everybody according as their rank requires and their merit demands; but nothing is more tedious than mere ceremony.

The possession and display of the easiest moral virtues will secure a more enviable popularity than the exhibition of the greatest talents without them. The ability to employ power well is the best sort of power, therefore taste in conversation is worth more than talent. Avoid opposition and argument in conversation, and be as willing to hear as to speak, and never interrupt the one speaking, nor affect to help him through with his discourse. Notice what is unpleasant in others, and avoid it; notice what gives you pleasure, and practice it, adopting the golden rule to all the minor affairs of life. There are those who in society are considerate, amiable, and really polite, who in private and at home are morose, rough, and ill-natured. This fault is much too common, and is one of the greatest inconsistencies of human nature. From the world they procure but a few moments' pleasure; but home is to yield the happiness of a whole life. The forms and ceremonies of politeness may be dispensed with in a measure, in the relaxations and intimacies of one's own fireside, but kind attentions never.

The duties of hospitality are of frequent occurrence and should never be omitted, even though fatiguing and sometimes troublesome. Those who are willing to dispense with them give occasion for unfavorable remark, and acquire the reputation of a want of delicacy, of a correct education, and a destitution of those kindly feelings, which are the charm of society, and also fail in one of the loveliest of Christian duties. Selfishness and pride are the two greatest obstacles in the way of a correct deportment; the former must be banished from social life as utterly inconsistent with the practice of those virtues and graces that adorn the human character and elevate man to his true position; the latter never finds a place in the manners of the truly well-bred, and is as much at variance with the laws of etiquet as of religion.

Extract from George Washington's Code of Manners, from *Rules of Civility & Decent Behavior in Company and Conversation: a Book of Etiquette,* written in his early youth—"Every action in company ought to be with some sign of respect to those present. Be no flatterer, neither play with anyone that delights not to be played with. Read no papers, letters, or books in company. Come not near the papers or books of another so as to read them. Look not over another when he is writing. Let your countenance be cheerful, but in serious matters be grave. Show not yourself glad at another's misfortunes. Let your discourse with others on matters of business be short. It is good manners to let others speak first. Strive not with your superiors in argument, but be modest. When a man does all he can, do not blame him, though he succeeds not well. Take admonitions thankfully. Be not hasty to believe flying reports to the injury of another. In your dress be modest, and consult your condition. *Play not the peacock, looking vainly at yourself.* It is better to be alone than in bad company. Let your conversation be without malice or envy. Urge not your friend to discover a secret. Break not a jest where none take pleasure in mirth. Speak not injurious words either in jest or earnest. Gaze not on the blemishes of others. When another speaks be attentive. Be not apt to relate news. Be not curious to know the affairs of others. Speak not evil of the absent. When you speak of God, let it be with reverence. Labor to keep alive that spark of heavenly fire called conscience."

ADDITIONAL RULES

Avoid in company all unnecessary noise or motion. Lean not your chair against the wall or furniture. Spit not upon the carpet or floor. Neither whistle nor hum tunes in company, nor drum with your feet or fingers. There should be a steady resistance of everything vulgar, and if the customs of society are such as to induce a violation of principle, or have an unfavorable influence on character, even remotely, it is then a duty to refuse politely, but resolutely, all participations in such practices or customs. Never fear to be singular in doing *right*, as this is one of the first essentials of good breeding.

MORAL EFFECTS OF DRESS—PROPRIETY

A wise man in giving advice to his students enforces the importance of personal neatness and suitable attention to dress, as having an important influence upon the taste and habits of the mind. It is no less important in this particular than in producing self-respect, and in securing the respect of others. Attention to the minor articles of attire, far more than its richness and elegance, affect the mind favorably. No one should be wholly inattentive to his personal appearance; and none should be so devoted to dress and fashion as to betray a weakness of intellect or the want of a well balanced mind. "She who spends too much time in consulting her mirror will assuredly spend too little in looking into her own heart, and she may safely calculate that the most finished external adorning will fail to please when the inward ornaments of intellectual and moral worth are neglected and forgotten." Still as a fine picture derives additional beauty from judicious framing, so the charms of an accomplished woman become enhanced by a proper regard to her attire; but the slave of fashion is perhaps one of the most pitiable objects in creation; and nothing can be more absurd than the adoption of every new style of dress the moment it makes its appearance.

The true standard of propriety is a medium one—neither adopt every rising novelty of the day, nor reject a consistant and becoming compliance with those alterations and changes which reflection and judgment pronounce desirable. Neatness, taste, and simplicity should be the characteristics of attire, which may always be adapted to the station in life. Due attention should also be paid to the seasons, and adaptation in dress should reflect the weather, as it betokens a culpable ignorance as well as egregious folly to be unseasonably attired. When the *real* or *supposed* demands of fashion involve a sacrifice of health, or endanger life, let the mandate be sternly and *rigorously* resisted and contemned.

TRAINING OF INFANTS—PROTECTION FROM COLD, ETC.

The exposure of infants to a low temperature, whether from deficient or improper clothing, will prove injurious to them. It has been ascertained that out of one hundred children born in winter, sixty-six die in the first month of life, but of one hundred born in summer, only seventeen die during the first month. Also, that the mortality is greater among children born in northern climates than in those born in southern climates. From these facts it is evident that infants should be furnished with a greater amount of clothing than adults. Nothing is more common, however, than to see children with their arms, necks, and upper portions of the chest bare. When we reflect on the close sympathy between the skin and internal organs of the body, we may easily decide on the probable cause of disease in the liver, lungs, stomach, bowels, and brain; and hence croup, catarrh, fever, diarrhea, cholera, and convulsions are but parts only of that wide outlet to infant life that deficient clothing creates. Some justify this course with the impression that it inures to cold and makes them hardy. This may be the case with those who have stamina sufficient to survive the experiment, but before

the system is thus invigorated, the child may be carried off by some inflammatory affection produced by such exposure.

INFANT NURSING

To set a child quite upright before the end of the first month is hurtful. Afterwards it may be done by degrees. Rubbing a child all over with the warm hand takes off the scurf and makes the blood circulate. Rubbing the ankle bones and inside the knees will strengthen those parts.

POSITION

A nurse should keep the child in her arms as little as possible, lest the legs should be cramped and the toes turn inward. The oftener the posture is changed the better; do not let it lie always on one side, nor let it lie too long even if it is quiet.

EXERCISE

By slow degrees the infant should be accustomed to exercise, both within doors and in the open air; but it should not be moved about much after feeding; it is apt to sicken. Exercise must be gentle, not jolting on the knee.

PREVENT DISTORTION

Tossing a child and exercising it in the open air

in fine weather is of great service. In cities, especially, children must not be kept in hot rooms, but must have as much air as possible. Want of exercise is the cause of rickets, large heads, weak joints, a contracted breast, and diseased lungs, besides a numerous train of other evils.

Infants should by imperceptible degrees be inured to a cool and then to a cold bath. Sudden transitions are dangerous. All attempts to render them hardy must be made by gradual steps. But when they become accustomed to a hardy system, it then must be adhered to.

CLEANLINESS

The child's skin must be kept perfectly clean, by washing its limbs morning and evening, and likewise its neck and ears, beginning with warm water, and by degrees it will not only bear but like to be washed in cold water. After carefully drying the whole body, head, and limbs, another soft cloth, a little warm, should be used gently, to take all the dampness from the folds and fleshy parts. If the skin is chafed, the nursery powder must be dusted on. The utmost tenderness is necessary in drying the head, and no binding should be made close about it. Squeezing the head or combing it roughly may cause frightful diseases and even the loss of reason. A small soft brush lightly applied is safer than a comb. Clean clothes every morning will tend greatly to a child's health and comfort. The scurf that sometimes appears on the head should be oiled at night, well washed with soap and water in the morning, and gently combed.

DRESS

Wrap them in a shirt with a breadth of flannel open in the front and with a waist to tie in front that is longer than their feet; then wrap a petticoat of flannel over the shirt, with a waist that ties behind; finally, put a robe or frock over the petticoat, fastened in the back. Caps may be worn one, two, or three months, but not longer. The dress for night should be as for the day, except the petticoat is left off and night gown worn instead.

THE OPERATION OF DRESSING

The most tender care should be observed in moving the infant and turning it, that it shall not feel fatigue. The clothes should all be tied on, and so loose that two fingers may be inserted between the clothes and body. Bandages are forbidden. Idiotism and deformity are often owing to tight bandages.

SLEEP

Infants cannot sleep too long; it is well when they can enjoy a calm and long-continued rest, of which they should by no means be deprived, as this is the greatest support granted them by nature. A child lives comparatively much faster than an adult; its blood flows more rapidly, and sleep promotes more uniform circulation and facilitates digestion, while a horizontal position is favorable to growth and development. Still, sleep should be proportioned to the age. After six months, the time of sleep can be regulated. An infant should always sleep the whole night in preference to the day, and, as it grows older, a few hours morning and afternoon; and, after a while, to sleep after dinner will be sufficient. After a child is four or five years old, its time of sleep may be shortened one hour every succeeding year, so that a child of seven will not require to sleep more than eight or nine hours.

WAKING SUDDENLY

To awaken a child with a noise, or in an impetuous manner, is extremely injudicious and hurtful; nor should it be carried from a dark room into a glaring light, for the sudden impression of light debilitates the organs of vision, and lays a foundation for weak eyes from early infancy.

RESTLESSNESS AT NIGHT

An infant is sometimes restless at night; this is generally owing either to cramming it with too much food, tight night-clothes, or being over-heated with too many blankets, or it may have slept too much in the daytime.

HICCUPS

These generally arise from acidity in the stomach, and may be remedied by a little prepared chalk given in a little syrup or gruel. If very severe, the stomach should be rubbed with opodeldoc or liniment, with a little laudanum added.

EXCORIATIONS

If children are not kept perfectly dry, or if their clothes are dried too long and become rough, they suffer much, and often they become perfectly raw about the thighs. When this is the case, the citron or yellow ointment will heal very soon. But "prevention" is far better than "cure"; great care should therefore be taken that suffering of this kind is not caused by inattention or carelessness.

HABITS OF INFANTS

There should be pains taken to form such habits in infancy as will be most for the child's benefit and least trouble to those who have the care of them. It is fatiguing and irksome to be obliged either to bear the fretfulness and screams of a child, or to walk the room continually to pacify it. There is no habit sooner learned than that of being carried in the arms; it needs only be practised a few times, and it becomes necessary for the enjoyment of quiet and peace. Having a light at night is also bad, it must soon be dispensed with, or it will become necessary to continue it. Keeping a child up in the evening is also injudicious. Let it be early prepared for rest, and you will have the benefit of a quiet evening, and your child of needful sleep and a well-formed habit.

WALKING

Let a child gain strength in the natural use of its limbs, not urging it beyond its strength to make efforts to walk. Let it practise creeping, occasionally holding it up to learn the use of the feet. But by no means stress it to go alone too soon. I have seen children have a natural stoop that could never be overcome in consequence of walking too soon, before there was sufficient strength to support the weight.

TEMPER

The atmosphere in which an infant should live should be that of gentleness. Nothing harsh or loud should ever fall upon the delicate ear of the infant. Nothing unkind or unfeeling should be made to vibrate upon its susceptible heart. It should hear no other tones than those of love and tenderness, and should feel no other influences than those of the deepest affection. Its upward turned eye is quick to discover the meaning of the look and manner, and its emotions are taking their hue from the light under which it lives and breathes. When symptoms of temper in the child are betrayed, let no exciting cause perpetuate the difficulty, but endeavor to change the current of thought by changing its place, or placing before the eye something to please, and calm the ruffled waters of its narrow but treasured life.

Chapter 3: SIMPLE AND SAFE REMEDIES FOR COMMON DISEASES AND ACCIDENTS

CHILBLAINS

These sores are caused by frost and are very troublesome, and often painful. Where the skin is not broken, bathe the part in strong alum water. This will cure, if continued a week or two.

BLEEDING AT THE NOSE

Grate dried salt beef, and take two or three pinches as snuff. This is said always to cure. Other remedies will often suppress it—such as the following: Raise the left arm, and keep it up some time. Bathe the back of the head and neck in cold water. Tie a thread very tight around the little finger.

WARTS

Wet them with tobacco juice, and rub them with chalk. You can also rub them with fresh beef every day until they begin to disappear. This last is simple and effectual.

CORNS

Take half an ounce of verdigris, two ounces of beeswax, two ounces of ammonia; melt the two last ingredients together, and just before they are cold, add the verdigris. Spread it on small pieces of linen and apply it, after paring the corn. This has cured inveterate corns.

FOR A STING

Bind on the place a thick plaster of common salt or saleratus moistened—it will soon extract the venom.

RING WORMS

Take tobacco and boil it well—add vinegar and lye, and wash often. Gunpowder and vinegar is also good. You can also lay a penny in a spoonful of vinegar, and, after standing a few hours, wash it frequently. This will cure.

RICKETS

Keep the bowels regular—bathe the body in tepid salt and water. Friction, air, exercise, and nutricious diet are important.

FOR RINGWORM AND SCALD HEAD

Give cream of tartar and sulphur, sufficient to act upon the bowels. Wash the head with fine soap and water, and apply the citron or yellow ointment once a day. Also simmer a decoction of elder with cream, until an ointment is formed, and apply daily—washing as above and taking the cream of tartar and sulphur.

Another method is to take of sulphate of potash, recently prepared, three drachms; Spanish white soap one drachm and a half; limewater seven ounces and a half; spirits of wine two drachms. Mix, by shaking well in a phial. Bathe the head a few times, morning and evening, and it will soon heal, without shaving the head.

SALT RHEUM

One quart of vinegar to a quarter of a pound of litharge, boiled down to half a pint. When settled, turn it carefully from the sediment. Take a stick, round at the end, and stir in two ounces of sweet oil, or more, until it has a consistency thicker than cream. This has cured very bad cases. Remedies for the blood should always be given while healing any cutaneous disease.

THE ITCH

To the above, add one scruple of red precipitate, and the same quantity of pulverized sal-ammonia, and it is an infallible remedy for this dreaded and loathsome disease.

It is scarcely necessary to give any caution on this subject. It is not difficult to cure, and is never a primary disease, only among the lowest and uncleanly of the poor, but is imparted by contact.

A CREAK, OR PAINS IN THE BACK, SIDE, SHOULDER, ETC.

Spread a plaster of brown hard soap on a cloth, wet it over with volatile liniment, and sprinkle it well with cayenne pepper, and it will relieve entirely in a day or two.

POLYPUS

Take pulverized bloodroot and bayberry, equal parts, and use it as snuff. If the passage is nearly closed, take a small swab, wet and dip it into the snuff, and touch the diseased part as far up as possible.

MORTIFICATION

Apply poultices of yeast, thickened, if convenient, with flour of slippery elm, warm and renewed often, giving the patient a glass of yeast three or four times a day and tonic bitters.

FOR SPRAINS AND BRUISES, WHEN THE SKIN IS NOT BROKEN

Take a pint of soft soap, a handful of salt, a tablespoon of saltpeter, powdered, and apply to the part affected with a bandage.

FELON

Take blue flag-root and wild turnip, a handful of each, stewed in half a pint of hog's lard and strained. Add four teaspoons of tar, and simmer them together. Apply this ointment until it breaks. Add beeswax and rosin to the ointment, for a salve, to dress it with after it breaks. This is an infallible cure, without losing the joint. The root of the fleur-de-lis, the Iris of our gardens, boiled soft, mashed fine, and with a little meal or flour to make a poultice, is another safe and sure remedy. The poke-root is said to be equally good. These remedies are safe, and have given relief and affected cures.

SIMPLE AND PERFECT CURE FOR A BURN

Take essence of peppermint and whiskey, in proportions of one part peppermint and three parts spirits, and apply with cloths; it gives perfect relief, instantly. Peppermint and sweet oil is equally good, put on with cotton. This should be always at hand, whenever there is danger from such accidents, as it acts like a perfect charm, and will not fail to relieve.

ACID STOMACH

Prepared chalk, to be found always at druggists, is an excellent remedy for this complaint, and all the unpleasant headaches and sickness to which it gives rise. This is one form of dyspepsia, and is sometimes relieved by the use of this simple remedy.

STOP THE BLEEDING OF A WOUND

Lay lint on the orifice; lint; if that is not sufficient, put on flour and then lint.

CUTS

Bind on brown sugar until it ceases bleeding, then apply any common healing salve, with sugar melted in it; this takes out the soreness, better than the salve alone.

FOR WOUNDS

Wounds occasioned by anything that would produce lockjaw, such as nails, needles, etc., bathe with lye or pearlash water, and bind on a rind of pork. Spirits of turpentine is also good. Soft soap and salt, or chalk kept moist, is also a preventive for this dangerous disease. If from neglect this disease has been occasioned, without delay, you must give medicine to sicken the stomach, and use a warm bath to relax the nerves, and an anodyne once every four hours. If it does not yield to this treatment, and the jaw is so fixed that remedies cannot be taken, then give injections, with the addition of a strong tea of ipecac, and from a half ounce to an ounce of laudanum.

A SALVE FOR CUTS AND SORES

One ounce and a half of olive oil, two ounces of white liaculum, and two ounces of beeswax, melted together.

AGUE IN THE FACE

A plaster made of brown hard soap and brown sugar, mashed together, spread as a plaster, and applied, is an excellent remedy when the inflammation is great and will soon relieve. But a preventive and a remedy, in the commencement of this disease, is bathing the face with strong camphor, and applying volatile liniment to the gums, and getting the face and ear warm as soon as possible. Ginger poultices are also good.

RHEUMATISM

A simple tea of gum guiac and queen of the meadow gives often great relief in chronic rheumatism, and in weakness of the limbs.

EXCORIATIONS AND SORES

For sores that will not heal with common remedies, use the citron or yellow ointment, two or more times a day, at the same time taking cleansing remedies for the blood. This often heals in a short time, when the skin is nearly off, in a single day or night, and acts like a charm. It may be found at the druggists.

DEAFNESS

Take five drops of sassafras oil and half an ounce of sweet oil and mix and drop into the ear, once or twice a day. A solution of kreosote is also recommended, the only sensation produced being an agreeable warmth.

TIC DOLOUREUZ

The Belladonna pill sometimes gives great relief; taken once in four hours. Apply to a physician or druggist for the article. Sometimes a mustard poultice will answer.

HYDROPHOBIA

Wash and cleanse the wound, and apply to every part of it the nitrate of silver, commonly called lunar caustic. This destroys the poison on the surface of the wound, which will come away. If the wound be deep, the caustic should be pointed to reach every part. If faithfully applied, a celebrated physician declares the patient perfectly safe.

CHAPPED LIPS AND HANDS

Take equal parts of beeswax and rosin, or Burgundy pitch, mutton tallow, or sweet oil, enough to make a soap or ointment; you may add a little rose water. This occasionally applied will relieve soon.

TO PREVENT BRUISES FROM TURNING BLACK

Make a plaster of salt and tallow to cover the wound.

STIFF JOINTS

Take strong salt and water (or brine), beef's gall, one gill each, and four yolks of eggs beat up; mix and shake them well together, and apply three times a day. Discutient ointments are also effective.

BOILS

Make a plaster of molasses and flour, or honey and flour, and apply it as often as they get dry. If very painful, make a soft poultice of bread and milk, moistened with volatile liniment and laudanum. This will ease pain, allay inflammation, and hasten a cure. Remedies for cleansing the blood should be freely used.

TO REMOVE PROUD FLESH

Pulverize loaf sugar very fine, and apply it to the part affected. This is a new and easy remedy, and is said to remove it entirely, without pain. It has been practised in England for years.

CATARRH IN THE HEAD

Some recommend bathing the head and shoulders in cold water as a preventive, and also snuff made of equal parts of gum Arabic, gum myrrh, and bloodroot, pulverized. But a more simple remedy has sometimes given great relief. Snuff new milk morning and night, not omitting it. This is a common disease, and is one cause of consumption.

DROPSY

A pint of the ashes of hickory bark, put in a pint of wine, and used three times a day, in doses of a wineglass full, restored a patient who had given up the last hope of life.

BRONCHITIS

The application of one drop of Croton oil, rubbed on the throat daily, against the part affected, produces a singular but powerful eruption, which has restored entirely the tone and vigor of the voice. For the chronic kind, a pill of tar, loaf sugar, skunk-cabbage-root, pulverized and taken every two or three hours, daily, as it may agree with the stomach, has cured in five or six days.

CROUP

Dissolve half a teaspoon of ipecac in half a teacup of warm water. Sweeten it, and give a half or a whole teaspoon, according to the age, until vomiting is produced; then give it in smaller quantities, and less frequently. Wrap up the child to promote perspiration and bathe the throat with volatile liniment or tobacco ointment. The above will give relief in a short time, if taken in season. Onion juice and molasses may be given to vomit, but there should be no delay. It is known by a peculiar whistling sound in the breathing, and if neglected at all proves fatal.

PUTRID SORE THROAT

Take two tablespoons of Cayenne pepper and one teaspoon of salt to half a pint of boiling water; let it stand one hour, then add half a pint of warm vinegar. Dose one tablespoon every hour; use it also as a gargle. This has been proved infallible.

COMMON SORE THROAT

A simple gargle of salt, vinegar, pepper, and water, in proportions to make a pleasant combination, will cure a common soreness of the throat.

EARACHE

Cotton wool, wet with camphor, or paragoric and sweet oil, hot, and the ear bandaged will give relief.

MUMPS

Care should be taken to prevent taking cold. Perspiration should be promoted by warm drinks. If there is costiveness, give a gentle laxative. Cover the swelling with cotton, and if painful, bathe it with volatile liniment or Cheeseman's balsam.

You can also utilize Powdered alum and barley water, as a gargle. To inhale the steam of tansy, wormwood, hops, and vinegar, and to bind the hot herbs on the throat, is also good.

ERUPTIONS

Dissolve Epsom salts, and bathe the parts affected two or three times a day.

NIGHT SWEATS

Take fifteen or twenty drops of elixir vitriol, once or twice a day; take the last dose at night. Cold sage tea, or Virginia snake-root, may be substituted for the above occasionally.

SPINAL AFFECTIONS

Bathing in strong tepid salt and water is good for this and other bone diseases.

MEASLES

Bathe the feet in warm alkali, and the surface of the body also. If the eruptions should disappear, use measures to promote perspiration. Give a gentle laxative every day, while the symptoms continue. If there is restlessness at night, give a small Dover's powder; for nausea at the stomach, saleratus water, with a few drops of peppermint, will soon relieve.

WORMS IN CHILDREN

Make a strong sage tea, and dissolve in it a little sale ratus; sweeten it, and, if preferred, add a little milk. Salt and water is also good, especially if there are symptoms of fits.

CANKER IN THE MOUTH

Take half a teaspoon of gunpowder, and dissolve in two spoonsful of clear water. Roll up a clean cloth like a pipe-stem; lay one end in the dissolved gunpowder, and the other in a dry saucer; in a few hours, the same will contain a liquid as clear as the purest water; sweeten this thick with loaf sugar or honey, and with a soft swab touch the parts affected several times a day, which will very soon destroy the canker. It has been used for infants with success.

TO STOP VOMITING

A cloth wet in essence of peppermint, laid across the stomach, is good. A plaster made of pulverized cloves, ginger, vinegar, and Indian meal, and applied to the stomach, is also good. A small pill of cayenne pepper will sometimes stop it very soon.

BILIOUS CHOLIC

Take a teaspoon of saleratus, a teaspoon of laudanum, and half a pint of mint tea. Give a small tablespoon, every half hour, or as often as vomiting occurs, and when it is allayed, give a double portion of bilious pills, or some active physic. If the bowels are inactive, injections are the anchor of hope. If the pain is intense, they should be given at first, made as follows: To a pint of starch, add half a pint of molasses, a pint of milk, a wineglassful of sweet oil or fresh lard, and a teaspoonful of table salt. Give as much as the patient can bear every two hours, or until relief is obtained. A teaspoonful of laudanum may be added, if there is great pain. For a common cholic, take a teaspoon of Cayenne pepper and a teaspoon of sugar; pour on them a teaspoon of boiling water, and sip as soon as cool enough to drink. If necessary, give a dose of oil, or other physic.

CHOLERA MORBUS

Take a teaspoon each of saleratus, powdered cinnamon, and cloves; pour on them a pint of boiling water, and when nearly cold, add a spoonful of an anodyne injection, made of a pint of starch, half a gill of molasses, a spoonful of sweet oil, or lard, a teaspoon of salt, and half a teaspoon of laudanum.

DYSENTERY

This disease is entirely different from common diarrhea, and proceeds from different causes. It is inflammatory, and all stimulating remedies should be avoided. Mucilaginous drinks should be freely used; a pill of ipecac, and a small Dover's powder may be given alternately, once every two or three hours, as the case requires. A general moisture of the skin should be kept up, and, if there is much pain, give the above anodyne injection.

DIARRHEA

For an infant, mix a teaspoon of paragoric, with one of magnesia, add half a teacup of water, and sweeten it with loaf sugar. Give a teaspoon of this mixture once in two hours. To a child three or four years old give it at two doses. The diet should be light and mucilaginous. Scalded milk, or arrowroot are good. If it is chronic, and continues, make a syrup of a teaspoon of rhubarb, of cinnamon and cloves one each, steeped in half pint of water; strain, and add two teaspoons of prepared chalk; sweeten with loaf sugar. Dose—a teaspoon every hour.

PURULENT OF OPTHALMIA

In this affection, the discharge from the eyes is capable of communicating the disease if applied to a healthy person. The towels used by the patient, should not be used by others. And anyone attending another in this complaint, should be careful to wash his hands, after having washed their eyes, etc. In this disease, the patient should sleep alone.

ERYSIPELAS

This is known by diffuse swelling, accompanied with a red blush, or suffusion, on the face, arms, &c., which feel burning hot, and is attended with symptoms of fever. The apartment should be cool and well ventilated; the changes of linen frequent. If there should be appearance of matter, the nurse should cover any scratch with lard when touching the discharge, and immediately after she has been handling the parts, should wash her hands with soap and warm water. All the directions of the medical attendants should be strictly obeyed.

RINGWORM OF THE SCALP

Children who are affected with this complaint, should be separated from other children. It is a disease that is apt to resist remedies, but it may be cured with proper applications faithfully applied.

Infectious diseases are communicated through the air, some of the most common are the following:

WHOOPING COUGH

This disease should never be allowed to take its natural course, but should be treated with remedies appropriate to its distressing nature. Riding, well ventilated rooms, and mild and loosening syrups are very beneficial.

SCARLET FEVER

Requires a cool apartment, very free ventilation, and frequent changes of linen The nurse should be one who has had this disease.

MEASLES

They require a warm, or at least a temperate apartment free from currents of air; sudden changes of heat and cold are dangerous. Clean linen should be carefully aired. The diet, farinaceous; the beverage, toast water.

SMALL POX

In this loathsome disease, the apartment should be large, cool, and well ventilated. The windows should be open day and night, and the linen changed daily. During the discharge of the pustules, change it twice a day. The patient should be taken into the open air often. Children and others, even if they have been vaccinated, should not visit the sick-room, though they need not leave the house. After the disease is over, the bed and bedding should be scoured, the room fumigated and thoroughly cleansed.

TYPHUS FEVER

If the apartment is large, airy, and clean, there is little danger from infection. The simple process spoken of in another part of this work will prevent any bad effect from the disease. The sheets and body linen should be change once or twice in twenty-four hours, and instantly removed from the room, as well as all evacuations. Chloride of lime, or common lye, should be used in the night-chair or bedpan. It is well also to use it in washing the clothes.

CONSUMPTION

The apartment should be large and well ventilated, but the temperature mild and equable as possible, about 65° Fahrenheit. The diet should be light, mostly vegetable and farinaceous. The invalid should take moderate exercise, either in a carriage, or on horseback, sailing or swinging; exercise should be taken within doors. This disease, by many, is thought to be contagious. On the Island of Cuba, they have a law that furniture and clothing, when there is a fatal termination, shall be destroyed, the walls to be removed and newly plastered. This we think unnecessary, but it is well to cleanse the air, and use precautions in the preservation of health during any case of fatal sickness.

When contagious or infectious diseases occur in a family, there should be no yielding to fear or alarm. The mind should be calm, and as undisturbed as possible, as the depressing passions render a person very susceptible to the poison of contagion or infection. The diet should be more generous than usual, and disinfecting agents should be frequently used. Cleanliness in every respect, and ventilation, are indispensable. By such management and precaution, diseases of these classes rarely extend.

INFLAMMATORY DISEASES

Except when the chest is the seat of disease, the temperature should be rather low or cool. Directions are generally given by the medical attendant, but when this is not the case, it may be laid down as a general rule to avoid giving animal food, wine, spirits, porter, or any stimulants in this class of complaints. Liquid food is most suitable, narrow root, toast-water, etc. The medical treatment in such diseases is more active than in others, and as they run their course rapidly, very much depends on strict attention to the direction of the physician. Ill-judged tenderness and indulgence should never spare the invalid child its dreaded and nauseous dose, for its precious life may depend upon its being faithfully administered. Care should be taken when the patient is partially recovered, not to bring in a relapse by over eating, indulgence in improper food, and over exertion. He should proceed timidly and gradually in renewing all his former habits and employments.

DISEASES OF DEBILITY

Under this term may be comprehended all those various and often chronic diseases that originate chiefly from a disordered state of the digestive organs, and a deranged and impaired state of the nervous system. They have more or less influence on the mind and require peculiar management. Everything should be done to promote cheerfulness, and to encourage hope in the invalid; it does good like medicine, and medicine does little good without it. The most careful attention should be paid to diet, clothing, and exercise, and the mind kept as much as possible from dwelling on desponding subjects. Let them understand that it is a part of the disease to apprehend the worst, and in every new pain to fear a new disease. This will give the mind repose, and allay its apprehension, preparing the way for recovery.

HINTS FOR NURSING THE SICK

The person who acts as nurse, should be present during the doctor's visit to the patient, and should help the sick in giving account of himself. Exactness and punctuality in following prescriptions is indispensable; no one should be employed who would not make it a point of conscience. There should always be a time-piece at hand, that different doses may not interfere with each other. Nothing should be concealed from the physician that is important for him to know. The countenance should wear a cheerful expression, and all the movements should be gentle and noiseless as possible in a sick room.

It is rarely proper to wake a patient for anything, as sleep is often more useful than medicine, and should never be done unless the physician deems it necessary. Never burden the sick with officious and unmeaning attentions, and never let them feel the want of care.

Trifles that would not disturb the mind of one in health, will often annoy, and even distress the invalid; the clatter of renewing the fire, the careless opening and shutting of doors, all harsh movements, should be studiously avoided.

Great care should be used in preventing colds in changing the linen, and in removing the patient from one bed or another. Chills are often a consequence of a cold fresh bed when a little care would have prevented it. A flannel sheet to wrap around the person is a great safeguard, especially if there are no conveniences for warming the bed. The linen should be well aired and warmed, before being used, and then the utmost caution is necessary in preventing chills from the external air, which has often been the cause of much suffering. A blanket or shawl should be constantly at hand to put around the shoulders when sitting up in bed. Let a towel be spread over the sheet, when the food or liquids are taken, to prevent untidiness. The bedclothes should be straightened and the pillows smoothed frequently; it is refreshing to the weary and often restless sufferer.

If you are only a watcher for the night, be sure to understand the directions for food and medicine, and omit nothing. Take care of your own health by being warmly clad during the chillness of night, and if the patient requires air, protect yourself from its influence. Have the sick room quiet at an early hour, with things so arranged that but little movement shall be necessary through the night. Do not refuse to take refreshment; plain food supplies the place of sleep to the exhausted body, and helps one to keep awake. When friction is used have mittens made of flannel and tied around the wrist, it is more convenient for the nurse and more soothing to the patient. When hot fomentations are needed, dip the cloth in the hot water, and fold it in a cool towel, wringing both together to prevent turning the hands. Feverish patients are greatly refreshed by sponging the hands, face, and feet with tepid water. When the feet are to be bathed in warm water, add hot water as fast as it cools, and when bathed long enough, wipe one at a time with a warm dry towel, and cover with a woollen stocking. In dressing a blister, have everything ready before the operation is commenced, as the ail is as painful as a burn, and when you have opened the lower part of the blister and let out the water, cover it as quickly as possible with wilted leaves or salve. Keep everything about the patient's bed and room perfectly clean; one *"keep clean* is worth ten *make clean."* Fresh air is of vital importance, and great pains should be taken to change it often, as well as to purify it. When you nurse the sick never allow your patience or self-possession to get exhausted; but let this thought cheer you in what you do. It is better to be the nurse, than the patient. If you discover infirmities of temper in the invalid, learn to avoid similar faults when you are equally tempted and are suffering yourself.

But above all other considerations, remember that you are helping to detain a soul from its final destiny, and that although the tenement is the special object of attention, let not the more important part be forgotten or neglected. Be alive to every word, look, or gesture that indicates the wants of the deathless spirit. Reading a portion of the Bible or some spiritual work, adapted to the occasion, may be rendered of infinite service to one shut out from the cares of the world, under the discipline that is designed for the improvement of the spiritual life.

Suffer not your own natural diffidence on such subjects to deter you from eliciting confidence or imparting and securing instruction for the soul struggling to be free.

A FEW CHOICE MEDICAL RECEIPTS

OPODELDOC

Take common white soap, three ounces; camphor, one ounce; oil of origanum, half an ounce; alcohol, one pint. Cut the soap and dissolve it in the alcohol, in which the other articles had been previously dissolved, and cool in wide-mouthed vials for use.

PARAGORIC

Take opium: one drachm; flowers of benzoin, one drachm; camphor, two scruples; oil of anise, one drachm; liquorice, one ounce; spirits, one quart. Dose, a teaspoon for an adult; half of a teaspoon for a child two years old.

DR. ROBERT'S WELCH MEDICA MENTUM

Gum aloes, half an ounce; rhubarb, one ounce; ginger, one ounce; myrrh, one drachm; Cayenne pepper, one teaspoon; spirits, one quart. Steep twenty-four hours, then add a teacup full of sugar and half pint of water. Take from one to two large tablespoons half an hour before eating. This is good for dyspepsia and other stomach derangements, and is a good family medicine for children as well as females.

Having used this simple and invaluable medicine for more than twenty years, I can tell all to try it. —D. Newell

SEIDLITZ POWDERS

Fold in on paper one drachm of Rochelle salts; in a blue paper, fold a mixture of twenty grains of tartaric acid and twenty-five grains of carbonate of soda. They should all be pulverized very fine. Dissolve their contents in separate tumblers not half full of water, then pour the one into the other, it will effervesce immediately. Drink while foaming.

SODA WATER

Take one third of a teaspoon of carbonate of soda and half that quantity of tartaric acid; add loaf sugar to make it pleasant. Dissolve the soda first, and drink while it foams.

FOR ELIXIR PROPRIETATIS

One ounce of saffron, one ounce of myrrh, and one ounce of aloes; pulverize them, and let the myrrh steep in a half pint of rum or brandy for four days; then add the saffron and aloes; let it stand where it is warm, and shake it well twice a day for a fortnight. This given to children, a teaspoon once a month, will prevent their being troubled with worms, and it is also good for adults occasionally.

HEALING SALVE

Take equal parts of rosin, beeswax, and sweet oil; melt and mix, stirring until cool. This is a good healing salve for all common sores, but if a more healing remedy is needed, add to this when almost boiling hot, two pounds of red lead; when almost cold, add half an ounce of pulverized camphor. This should be spread thin and renewed once or twice a day.

RHEUMATIC TINCTURE

Take camphor, two drachms; gum guiacum, one ounce; nitre, one ounce; balsam Tolu, two drachms; spirits, one quart; mix well. Dose: half a teaspoon in a little water three or four times a day.

TINCTURE FOR SPASMS—CRAMP IN THE STOMACH, ETC.

Take four ounces of camphorated spirits; four ounces of essence of peppermint; half an ounce of spirits of ammonia; one teaspoon of Cayenne pepper; two teaspoons of ginger. Dose: according to age and urgency of disease. One tablespoon every quarter, half, or one and two hours. It must be diluted with a little water and sweetened if preferred. This is valuable in sudden sickness.

SIMPLE MIXTURE FOR ALL BOWEL COMPLAINTS

Take rhubarb, one ounce; saleratus, one teaspoon; pour on them a pint of boiling water. When cold, add two teaspoons of essence of peppermint. Dose as above.

BLACKBERRY SYRUP

Take two quarts ripe black berries, one pound of loaf sugar, half an ounce of nutmeg, half an ounce of cinnamon, one quarter of an ounce of cloves, the same of allspice; boil all together for a short time, and when cold, add one pint of brandy. Strain and bottle. Dose: from a teaspoon to a wine glass full, three or four times a day. This by some is considered a specific in summer complaints.

URINARY MIXTURE

Take acetate of potash, two drachms; honey, half an ounce; spirits of turpentine, half a drachm; carbonate of soda, half a drachm; peppermint essence or tea according to the taste. Dose: two tablespoons three times a day. Gum Arabic to be taken in connection. This is good in cases of obstructions.

SYRUP FOR PURIFYING THE BLOOD

Take six pounds of sarsaparilla, three ounces of gum Guiacum, two pounds of the bark of sassafras root, two pounds of elder flowers, two pounds of burdock root, and add one gallon of cheap spirits and one gallon of water; boil and pour off the liquor repeatedly until all the strength is obtained. Boil down to six quarts; add fifteen pounds of sugar or more to make a syrup. Dose: a wine glass three or four times a day. Add to each bottle half a teaspoon of saleratus. The tea of yellow dock and burdock are also good.

VOLATILE LINIMENT

Take one ounce of spirits of ammonia or hartshorn, and add sweet oil until it is as thick and looks like cream This is good for an external application in all swellings and inflammation.

BALSAM OF HONEY

Take of balsam of Tolu, two ounces; gum storax, two drachms; opium, two drachms; honey, eight ounces. Dissolve these in a quart of spirit of wine. This balsam is very useful in hoarseness, and allaying irritations of the lungs. It will often cure a cough that is alarming.

GODFREY'S CORDIAL

Dissolve half an ounce of opium and one drachm of oil of sassafras in two ounces of spirits of wine. Mix four pounds of treacle with one gallon of boiling water, and when cold mix together. This is the celebrated cordial so much used for children.

FOR TOOTHACHE PASTE

Take gum of opium, gum camphor, and spirits of turpentine, equal parts, rub them in a mortar to a paste. Put in the hollow of the tooth This, it is said, will cure and prevent teeth from ever aching.

COUGH SYRUPS

Take Iceland moss, two ounces; four poppy heads; four tablespoons of barley; put in three pints of water, boil down to two, and strain it. Add one pound of sugar. Dose: a tablespoon whenever the cough is troublesome. Another, boil down thoroughwort to a thick syrup, and sweeten with molasses. This cures when other remedies fail.

EYE WATER

Take half an ounce of white copperas and dissolve it in a pint of soft water. Wet the corners of the eye three or four times a day or every hour. You can also take white vitriol as large as a large pea, the same of salt, an ounce of water, and a small piece of opium. Use two or three times a day.

TINCTURE FOR WATERBRASH

Take of compound tincture of senna, eight ounces; tincture of balsam of Tolu, half an ounce. Mix and take a tablespoon every morning fasting. Anti-dyspeptic pills are also good.

VOLATILE PLASTER FOR WHITE SWELLINGS

Melt together in an iron ladle, or earthen pipkin, two ounces of soap, and half an ounce of litharge plaster When nearly cold stir in a drachm of salammoniac in fine powder; spread upon leather, and apply to the part affected.

OINTMENT FOR INFLAMED EYELIDS

Take of prepared calomel, one scruple; spermaceti ointment, half an ounce. Mix them well in a glass or marble mortar, and apply a small quantity to each corner of the eye every night and morning, and also to the edges of the lids. Take occasionally a dose of Epsom salts. If the above does not remove the inflammation, take acetated zinc, six grains; rose water, six ounces; mix and apply before the ointment is used. It is said that these remedies have succeeded in every case to which they have been applied.

PRESERVATION OF THE DEAD

The beneficial effects of this are experienced in the case of keeping bodies for the recognition of friends. A solution of alum in hot water, in the proportion of two pounds to a pint, is injected through the right carotid arteries and veins throughout the whole body. In summer three quarts of the solution are required, and in winter less. This is to preserve the body in its original state.

HERBS

All medicinal herbs should be gathered while in blossom, and before the frosts have injured them. They should be well dried, and then they will be much stronger if kept from the air.

The uses of the common herbs are too well known perhaps to need any directions. Thoroughwort is excellent for coughs, colds, and liver and stomach derangements. A tea of catnip is opening to the pores. Lettuce and motherwort are soothing and quieting to the nerves, and are for the nervous and wakeful an excellent drink. Hop-tea, with saleratus dissolved in it, is invaluable for all common and frequent headaches, derangement of the stomach by acidity, etc. It is a good plan to gather burdock and horseradish leaves and dry them. When dipped in hot water or vinegar they are good for agues, inflammations, pains, etc., applied externally.

POISONS

Every person ought in some measure to be acquainted with the nature and cure of poisons. Those affected by them are generally taken unawares, and their effects are often so sudden and violent as to admit of no delay. No great degree of medical knowledge is here necessary; the remedies for most poisons being generally at hand, or easily obtained, and their application easy.

ANTIDOTES

The first thing to be done when a person has swallowed poison is to ascertain what it is he has taken; next, to be speedy in resorting to appropriate remedies, and if one fails, to try others without loss of time.

ACIDS—OIL OF VITRIOL, AQUAFORTIS, SEA-SALTS, OXALIC ACID

Symptoms—Burning heat in the mouth and stomach, bad breath, an inclination to vomit, or vomiting various matters mixed with blood, hiccups, etc., so great pain in the bowels that not even the weight of a sheet can be borne, burning thirst, difficulty of breathing, etc. Remedies—Mix an ounce of calcined magnesia with a pint of water, and give a glass full every two minutes. If it is not at hand, use flaxseed tea, rice water, or water alone in large quantities until the former can be procured. If it cannot be obtained, dissolve an ounce of soap in a pint of water, and take a glass full every two minutes; chalk or whiting may be taken, and give injections of milk often. If the patient does not vomit, put him in the warm bath, bleed him freely, and apply blisters over the part pained. If the cramps continue, take a cup of common tea, an ounce of sugar, fifteen or twenty drops of laudanum every quarter of an hour. No nourishment but sweetened rice water is to be taken for several days. In these cases nothing should be given to cause vomiting.

ALKALIES

These substances produce the same effects as acids, causing dreadful convulsions. Remedies—Take two tablespoons of vinegar or lemon juice in a glass of water at once, and follow it up by drinking large quantities of soap and water; other treatment as in acids.

MERCURY, COROSIVE SUBLIMATE, RED PRECIPITATE, VERMILION

Symptoms—Constriction and pain in the throat, stomach, and bowels, vomiting, and convulsions. Remedies—Mix the whites of twelve or fifteen eggs with two pints of cold water, and give a glass full every two minutes, with as much milk as can be swallowed, and large doses of ipecacuanha. If after it is taken, the vomiting does not cease, repeat the same with the addition of more water. The warm bath, blisters, leeches, etc. may be used to relieve the pain and inflammation.

ARSENIC

Symptoms the same as in mercurial poisons. Remedies—Give large quantities of cold sugar and water, until a plentiful vomiting is induced, to assist which give ipecacuanha in considerable doses, and barley and rice water or flaxseed tea and milk should afterwards be employed. Oil is never to be used until the symptoms are abated, or the poison is ejected. Hydrated peroxide of iron has also been administered with perfect success. It is said to overcome the effects of the poison immediately.

COPPER

The symptoms from the swallowing of verdigris are nearly the same as those of the mercurial poisons. The great remedy is, large quantities of sweetened water; in addition, use all the means recommended for corrosive sublimate, etc.

LUNARCAUSTIC

Dissolve two tablespoons of table salt in two pints of water; a few glasses of this will induce vomiting. If not relieved, use flaxseed tea, and other remedies good for acids.

SALTPETER

Pursue the plan recommended for arsenic in the first directions.

LEAD

Dissolve a handful of Epsom or glauber salts in a pint of water and give it at once; after vomiting is produced, use sweetened water. If the symptoms continue, do as directed for acids.

POWDERED GLASS

Stuff the patient with thick rice pudding, bread, potatoes, or any other vegetable; then give five grains of tartar emetic to vomit him, after which use milk freely; injections, warm bath, and fomentations are not to be neglected.

OPIUM

Let a teaspoon of Cayenne pepper, or twice the quantity of black, be steeped in about half a teacup of boiling water; give a teaspoon as often as possible until the whole be down. Immediately after give an emetic; as soon as it operates freely the patient should take a little more of the Cayenne and a tablespoon or more of lemon juice or strong vinegar, kept in motion until danger is over. In an hour after taking the lemon juice, give a little broth or light nourishing food, well seasoned with Cayenne or black pepper. This simple process will always subdue the poison of opium or any other narcotic. Infants have been relieved and saved from an over dose of paragoric or laudanum, by giving a spoonful of vinegar immediately.

MUSHROOMS

Give the patient immediately, three grains of tartar emetic; twenty-five or thirty of ipecac; and an ounce of salts, dissolved in a glass of water; one third to be taken every fifteen minutes until he vomits freely, then purge with castor oil.

TOBACCO, HEMLOCK, NIGHT-SHADE—SPURRED RYE, ETC.

An emetic, as directed for opium. If the poison has been swallowed some time, purge with castor oil. After vomiting and purging, if still drowsy, bleed and give vinegar and water.

POISONOUS FISH

Give an emetic. If it has been eaten some time, give oil and injections. After these have operated, twenty drops of ether may be taken on a lump of sugar. Vinegar and water may then be given.

BITE OF A SNAKE—MAD DOG, ETC.

The moment a person is bitten, apply a ligature above the wound, and compressed lightly by winding it up with a stick, close as it can be borne. Cut out the wound, and then touch it with caustic or pour in turpentine. A decoction of Spanish flies and turpentine should be applied to the skin around the wound to excite inflammation and suppuration, which is highly important. As soon as it is cut, take off the ligature. If the patient is too timid to bear the knife, burn the wound freely with caustic, and put in cotton well moistened with the above. The discharge of matter should be kept up some time. The use of the chlorwerts in these cases is much used with water in France and Germany. Apply it twice a day with lint; and take, three times a day, from two drachms to an ounce.

FOREIGN SUBSTANCES IN THE THROAT

Persons are sometimes in danger of suffocation from fish bones, pins, etc. that stick in the throat. When this occurs, desire the patient to be perfectly still, open his mouth and look into it. If you can see it, endeavor to seize it with your thumb and finger, or a long slender pair of pincers. If it cannot be got up, or is not of a nature to do injury in the stomach, push it down with the handle of a spoon or a flexible round piece of whale bone, the end of which must be covered with a roll of linen or anything of the kind that may be at hand. If you can neither get it up nor down, place six grains of tartar emetic in the patient's mouth; as it dissolves it will make him excessively sick, and in consequence of the relaxation, the bone or whatever it may be, will descend into the stomach or be ejected from the mouth. If a pin, button, or other metalic pointed body, has been swallowed, give rice, or other pudding plentifully, to sheathe the stomach from danger.

DRY MORTIFICATION

This sometimes comes of itself without apparent cause. It attacks the toes of old people, and appears in small bluish or black spots, which spread. Place a blister over the spot, and give two or less grains of opium night and morning, and keep the bowels open by castor oil.

TO STOP THE BLEEDING OF WOUNDS

If the flow of blood is but trifling, draw the edges of the wound together with your hand, and hold them in that position some time, when it will frequently stop. If, on the contrary, it is large, of a bright red color, flowing in spirts, or with a jerk, clap your finger on the spot where it springs from, and hold it there with a firm pressure, while you direct someone to pass a handkerchief around the limb above the cut, and tie it in a hard knot. A cane or stick of any kind must be passed under the knot, and turned round and round, until the stick is brought down to the thigh, so as to make the handkerchief of considerable tightness. You may then take off your finger; if the blood still flows, tighten the handkerchief with a turn or two of the stick until it ceases. The patient may now be removed, taking care to secure the stick, without running any risk of bleeding to death by the way. This is merely to prevent bleeding fatally until a surgeon can be called. If the wound is too high in the limb to admit of the handkerchief, press on above the wound, with the hand or anything that is of a hard substance.

POISON FROM ANIMAL PUTRIDITY

It is not generally known that animal matter becoming putrid, under certain circumstances, is a virulent poison, capable of destroying life if taken into the circulation, applied to the stomach, or applied to an abraded surface. Scarcely a year passes but more or less valuable life is sacrificed in this way. The physician and student, from a prick, a scratch, or trifling sore, at which this poison has entered the system, in a post mortem examination, have experienced its fatal effects. It is equally true that the matter from Erysipelas and other sores, after death, have been the cause of the same evils.

Cheese, after having undergone certain change, becomes animal poison. Sausages may become so from being kept too long. Meat will also become hurtful in the same way, though boiling-hot water will arrest it, and it may be rendered safe by using saleratus in cooking it. As the result of experiment, it is found that putrifying muscle, or pus, if placed on a fresh wound, will cause disease and death. But boiling water or alcohol will render it innoxious.

WATER GRUEL

Mix two tablespoons of Indian or oat meal with three of water. Have ready a pint and a half of boiling water in a sauce pan or skillet, perfectly clean; pour this by degrees into the mixture in the bowl; then return it back into the skillet and place it on the fire to boil. Stir it, and let it boil nearly half an hour. Skim it, and season it with a little salt. If it is admissible, a little sugar and nutmeg renders it more palatable. Also, if milk is not forbidden, a small teacup of milk added to a pint of gruel, and boiled up once, makes a nice dish for an invalid.

MILK PORRIDGE

This is made nearly in the same way as gruel, only using half flour, and half meal, and half milk instead of water, It should be cooked before the milk is added, and only boiled up once afterwards.

ARROWROOT.

A tumbler of this may be made in two minutes if you have boiling water. Take a teaspoon of the powder, moisten it with a tablespoon of cold water, rub it smooth, add another of warm water, and stir it until it is perfectly smooth; then pour on boiling water, stirring it until it changes to a transparent substance. It may be seasoned simply with salt, or with lemon juice and sugar, or with sugar and nutmeg, with a little milk. It may be made thick as blanc mange, and eaten with cold cream and sugar.

BEEF-TEA

Take one pound of lean fresh beef cut thin, put it in a jar or wide mouthed bottle, add a little salt, place it in a kettle of boiling water to remain one hour, then strain it, and there will be a gill of pure nourishing liquid. Begin with a teaspoon and increase as the stomach will bear. This has been retained on the stomach when nothing else could be, and has raised the patient when other means have failed.

WINE WHEY

Take half a pint of new milk, put it on the fire and the moment it boils, pour in that instant two glasses of wine and a teaspoon of powdered sugar previously mixed. The curd will soon form, and after it is boiled, set it aside until the curd settles. Pour the whey off and add a pint of boiling water, and loaf sugar to sweeten to the taste. This may be drank in typhus and other fevers, debility, etc.

SAGO

To a teacup of sago, allow a quart of water. Let it soak two or three hours, then boil it with some lemon peel until it is a clear transparent jelly. Milk may be used. Powdered loaf sugar, cream, and nutmeg may be taken as sauce.

CALVES FEET BLANCMANGE

Put a set of calves feet nicely cleansed and washed into four quarts of water and reduce it by boiling to one quart; strain it and set it by to cool. When cold, take off all the fat, remove all the settlings at the bottom, and put to it a quart of new milk, with sugar to taste, and boil it a few minutes. If you wish to flavor it with lemon peel or cinnamon, do it before boiling; if with rose water, peach water, essence of lemon, do it after. When boiled ten minutes, strain it through a fine sieve into a pitcher, and stir it till it cools. When only blood warm, put it in moulds that have been wet with cold water, and let it harden. This is good for the sick or well.

PANADA

One of the most simple and least hurtful dishes for the sick is cracker panada. Take half a bowl of boiling water, two or three large lumps of loaf sugar, roll a Boston cracker into fine crumbs, and when put in the bowl, grate over a little nutmeg. It is very simple and palatable. If wine is given, a teaspoon improves it.

BREAD PANADA

Take off the crust and boil two slices of bread in a quart of water about five minutes. Then take out the bread and beat it smooth in a dish, mixing with it some of the water in which it was boiled. Put in sugar and nutmeg to your taste, and if allowed a small piece of butter.

CHICKEN JELLY

Cut a chicken into small pieces, bruise the bones, and put the whole in a stone jar and cover it close. Set the jar in a kettle of boiling water, and keep it boiling three hours Then strain off the liquid, and season it with a little salt, pepper, mace, etc., or with loaf sugar and lemon. Return the chicken to the jar and boil again, it will produce nearly as much as before of jelly. It can be made just as well of an old fowl.

OUSTARD EGG

When a patient can bear a raw egg, it is very strengthening. Beat it and prepare it with sugar, milk, and nutmeg, and, as a drink, it is delightful.

BREAD JELLY

Toast four slices of stale bread, until they are of a light brown, having first taken off the crust; lay the bread in two quarts of boiling water. Add if you please, two tablespoons of lemon-juice, and let the bread boil to a jelly. Strain and sweeten it, and flavor with lemon-peel or nutmeg. It is excellent for very sick persons, or young children.

TAPIOCA JELLY

Wash four tablespoons of tapioca, and soak it in water enough to cover it for five hours. Set a pint of boiling water on the fire, and stir into it the tapioca. Put in a stick of cinnamon or mace, and let the whole simmer gently. When thick and clear, mix two tablespoons of white sugar, half a tablespoon of lemon-juice, and half a glass of white wine, if the patient can bear it, and stir into the jelly; then turn it into cups.

RICE GRUEL

Take one spoonful of rice, a pint and a half of water, a stick of cinnamon or lemon-peel; boil it soft, and add a pint of new milk; strain it, and season with a little salt. If you make it of rice flour, mix one spoonful with a little cold water smoothly, and stir it into a quart of boiling water. Let it boil five or six minutes, stirring it constantly. Season it with salt, nutmeg, and sugar, and if admissible a little butter. If the patient bears stimulants, a little wine may be added.

CALVES' FEET BROTH

Boil two feet in three quarts of water until the water is half gone. Take off all the fat, season with a little salt, and, if suitable, a spoonful of white or port wine to a teacupful. This is nourishing and strengthening for an invalid. If a richer broth may be used, boil with the feet two ounces of veal, or beef, and a slice of bread, and a blade or two of mace.

CHICKEN, BEEF, OR VEAL BROTH

This is made by cutting up the chicken, or the lean of veal or beef, and putting in two spoonsful of washed rice, and boiling until tender. It may be used, if needed in haste, after boiling in less water about fifteen minutes, then filling it up and finishing. It should be put by in a bowl or pitcher covered, to keep for use. Warm it, and add crumbs of Boston crackers or bread a day or two old, with a little salt, and there is nothing more palatable for the sick.

TOAST—WATER

Take a thin slice of stale bread; toast it brown on both sides slowly and equally. Lay it in a bowl, pour on boiling water, and cover with a saucer to cool.

HOT LEMONADE

Cut up the whole of a lemon, rind and all, add one teacup of white sugar, and pour on boiling water. This is good for colds, and is a pleasant drink for the sick.

CANDIED LEMON OR PEPPERMINT FOR COLDS

Boil one pound and a half of sugar in a half pint of water till it begins to candy around the sides, put in eight drops of essence. Pour it upon buttered paper and cut it with a knife.

HINTS ON THE PRESERVATION OF HEALTH

WET CLOTHES

It is impossible for people who go out much to avoid sometimes being wet. But the danger may be lessened, if not wholly prevented, by changing them soon. When this cannot be done, they should keep in action until dry. Wet clothes obstruct the perspiration, and even the most healthy are not proof against their ill effects; they occasion fevers, rheumatism, and consumption. Wet feet also are injurious. The delicate should especially be cautious in this respect.

CHANGES IN THE ATMOSPHERE

With us the degrees of heat and cold are not only very different in the seasons of the year, but often change from one extreme to another, in the course of a few days, and sometimes in the course of one day. The best method of fortifying the body against the changes of the weather, is to be abroad every day. Those who keep within doors are most liable to catch cold. They become so delicate that the slightest changes affect them, and are frequently afflicted with pains, coughs, oppression of the breast, etc. The physical powers and feelings are affected often materially by the change from winter to spring, and many are in the practice of being bled, or taking cathartics. They may, by the advice of a physician, be sometimes useful, but they should never be practised as a habit. Exercise is particularly useful at this season; friction of the skin, comfortable and suitable clothing, will often prevent what is termed the "spring fever." Another thing, the more you give way to the feeling of low spirits or languor, the more power they gain over you. Go forth into the beautiful sunshine, and along the pleasant places where God has scattered His glories so bountifully, walk with a swift step, and breathe with delight the pure and balmy air of spring, and let the new sweet sights and sounds of nature leave their invigorating and healthful influence upon the soul and frame.

FRESH AIR

It is not in the power of all to command equal advantages in this respect, but clean apartments, and the free admission of air at suitable times, are very necessary in promoting health and cheerfulness. Exposure to currents of air at any time, especially when the body is heated, sudden transitions from heat to cold, or from cold to heat, sleeping in damp rooms, damp linen, etc., are causes of cold, and therefore highly deleterious.

UNWHOLESOME DIET

A precaution on this subject is a word to the wise, and, if heeded, will prevent the train of ills to which it gives birth. Those who have delicate, or dyspeptic stomachs, must be, in this respect, self-denying. When they have once suffered from any food that is indigestible, they should practise abstinence. Experience is the best teacher; still, a few articles may be specified as unsafe. Crude vegetables, hard-boiled eggs, oily substances, fresh fish, salt-dried meats, made dishes; in short, everything that creates acidity should be carefully avoided. Animal food, if of a digestible and mild quality, may be used, though meat suppers are injurious.

CLOTHING

Under all circumstances there should be an adaptation of the state and condition of the weather. But when the digestive organs are deranged, or in cases of debility, it is of great importance to maintain a due action of the skin. The clothing should be suited to this purpose, warm, but not heavy, and that worn next the skin should be flannel, summer and winter, though of a lighter texture in summer. Following these directions a worn and frail physical nature will endure much longer the inclemencies of our changing and variable climate. The dress, too, should fit, without fettering the body. Faintings, fits, and death may be caused by tight-dressing. It stops or impedes circulation, and is one of the primary causes of bad health and broken constitutions.

RULES FOR THE PROMOTION OF HEALTH

Rise early, and never sit up late, if it can be avoided. Wash the body every morning, and rub it dry with a rough towel, or else use friction ten or fifteen minutes with a flesh brush. Drink no spirits, wine, or fermented liquors, unless prescribed by a physician. Sleep in a room that has free access to the open air. Keep the head cool by bathing it every morning with cold water and abate feverish and inflammatory symptoms by persevering stillness. Correct symptoms of plethora and indigestion, by eating and drinking less for a few days. Never eat a hearty supper of animal food. Never let a candle or lamp smoke after it is extinguished. Air your churches, houses, and rooms. Let no decaying substances, animal or vegetable, remain in your cellars or about your dwellings. Be cheerful, and never allow yourself to lose self-possession, for an unhappy state of the mind will produce a corresponding unhealthiness of the body.

EXERCISE

There is no kind of exercise more beneficial than walking, as it gives a general action to the muscle of the body, but for valetudinarians riding on horseback, or in a carriage, is preferable. Travelling for health often does more for the feeble than medicine. The feeble should never exercise immediately after meals; it often produces heartburn, eructations, and vomiting; or if not, retards the regular digestion of food. Reading aloud is a healthy exercise for the lungs; to speak very loud, or to exercise the voice immediately after a meal, is hurtful to the lungs, as well as to the organs of digestion. Singing, in a remarkable degree, promotes the circulation of the blood. Sedentary artificers and mechanics, who sing at their work, contribute much to the preservation of their health.

FRICTION

One of the most gentle and useful kinds of exercise is, friction of the body with a piece of flannel or a flesh brush. This was in great esteem among the ancients, and is so at present in the East Indies. The whole body may be subjected to this mild, healthful operation, but the spine, the bowels, etc. should be most carefully attended to. Friction clears the skin, resolves stagnating humors, promotes perspiration, strengthens the fibres, and increases the warmth and energy of the whole body. For anyone who has not leisure to take sufficient exercise it is an excellent substitute, and highly important.

For palsy, rheumatism, indigestion, it is an excellent remedy. It may be performed in bed at night, or in the morning before rising, and should be continued some minutes at a time.

BATHING

The tepid bath seems the best adapted to the purposes of cleanliness and healthy exercise. To delicate females and young children it is of primary importance; at any rate, frequent ablutions should be practised, and the skin rubbed dry. The feet should be bathed as often as once or twice a week. This is a luxury, as well as a promoter of health. Deaths are often recorded from premature bathing. It produces cramps, and there cannot be too much caution used in this matter. Never allow it when the water and weather is cold.

TO PRESERVE EYESIGHT

Never sit long at a time in perfect darkness, nor exposed to a blaze of light. Sudden transitions are not good. Avoid reading small print, or straining the eyes by looking at minute objects. If the eyes are disordered, do not read by candlelight, nor at dusk. Never gaze on glaring objects; nor allow too much light in your sleeping apartment. The furniture, drapery, etc. should not be altogether white; and if the eyes are weak, there will be much advantage in having green for the prevailing color in your room. The short-sighted should accustom themselves to holding their book as far off as possible, and the longsighted as near as may be. Bathing the head, eyes, face, and neck, in cold water every morning, strengthens the eves, and is an excellent practice.

TO PRESERVE THE TEETH

To wash the mouth is serviceable, not only to keep the teeth clean, and thus to prevent decay, but in strengthening the gums, and making them adhere firmly to the teeth, which is of great importance in preserving them sound and secure. Use a brush mornings, and, when powder is necessary, the prepared chalk alone is good; or, if the gums are becoming spongy, a mixture of Peruvian bark with it is better. If tartar accumulates on the teeth, apply to a dentist.

HAIR

If the head is dry and feverish, and the hair husky, oil it occasionally it will preserve it in a more healthy condition, and prevent its becoming gray. If, on the contrary there is too much moisture and oil on the hair, and it comes out, wash the head with soap and water, and wet in brandy occasionally to strengthen the roots. Macassor oil is also good to strengthen the roots—made as follows: Take three quarts of common oil, half a pint of spirits of wine, and three ounces of bergamot; heat them together, and, when removed from the fire, add four small pieces of alkanet root; keep it covered closely several hours, then strain, and it is ready for use. Palma Christe oil, scented, brushed into the hair twice a day two or three months, promotes its growth, and is said to be valuable making it luxuriant.

TO PREVENT THE SPREADING OF CONTAGION

It cannot be too widely known that nitrous acid possesses the properties of destroying the contagion of typhus fevers and other malignant diseases. By the following simple process the gas may be procured with but little expense and trouble. Place a little saltpeter on a saucer, and pour on it as much oil of vitrol as will just cover it; a copious discharge of acid gas will instantly take place. The quantity may be regulated by the ingredients. This is very important in preserving health and preventing the spread of contagion.

WHEN TENDING TO ANIMALS

FOR SPRAINS AND BRUISES IN HORSES

Dissolve an ounce of camphor in eight ounces of spirits of wine. Then add one ounce of spirit of turpentine. One ounce of spirit of sal ammonia; half an ounce of oil of origanum; one large tablespoon of laudanum. Rub in a quarter of an hour with the hand four times a day.

COUGH IN HORSES

It is said that the small twigs of cedar chopped fine and mixed with their grain will cure a cough, and that has been used with complete success.

CURE FOR THE BLACK TONGUE

A handful of fine salt rubbed upon the tongue of a horse that has this disease, will effect a cure in two or three applications.

TO RELIEVE CHOKED ANIMALS

Take a flexible rod about four feet long, and three fourths of an inch in diameter, wind on the butt end, tow or cotton, and tie a rag over that and grease it. To keep the mouth open place a piece of hard wood one foot long, four inches wide, one inch thick with a hole bored in the center for the rod to pass through, and then push it gently down the throat, and it is said to be always effectual and to give immediate relief. It is also said that a round stick about the size and length of a rolling pin with a cord tied in the notches in the ends, placed in the animal's mouth and fastened to each horn, will, if allowed a little time, unchoke them and save the suffering creature from a lingering death.

WOUNDS ON CATTLE

The most aggravated wounds are easily cured with the yolk of eggs mixed with the spirits of turpentine. Bathe the part several times a day and the cure will be effected in forty-eight hours.

BLOATING IN CATTLE

A tablespoon of spirits of ammonia for an ox or a cow; a teaspoon for a sheep diluted with water.

Chapter 4: USEFUL COOKING HINTS FOR HOUSE-KEEPERS

Do everything in its proper time. Keep everything in its place. Mend clothes before washing, except stockings; they are best darned when clean. Wash all colored garments with hard soap, and do it as quick as possible. Flannels should be washed in hot suds, and rinsed in clean, soft, boiling water; to stand until cool enough to wring out, and they will not turn yellow nor shrink. A little bluing improves them.

Alum or vinegar is good to set the colors of red, green, and yellow; salt is good for blue. Before you wash, dip blues in salt and water, use alum after. If table cloths are stained with tea, coffee, or fruit, turn on them boiling water, and let them stand till the water is cold, or the color will never come out. Starch all kinds of calico but black; use potato water for black, as that will not show. If there are many in a family that wear black, save the water when potatoes are boiled for this purpose.

Sal Soda will bleach clothes very white, but used in large quantities is thought to injure the texture. One spoonful is enough to put in a kettle when you boil. It can be found at druggists in the country, at other stores for eight or ten cents per pound.

Save all your suds for gardens and plants, or to harden cellars and yards when sandy.

Poland and flour starch should be first wet with a little cold water and stirred smooth, then poured on boiling water gradually, stirring it constantly, and then boiled a few moments. Stir Poland, or muslin starch, with a spermaceti or hallow candle, and it will not stick to the iron and will be very smooth and much nicer.

Count your clothes pins, spoons, knives and forks, towels, handkerchiefs, etc. every week.

Never pour boiling water on tea trays; wash them with cool suds, and polish with a little flour and dry cloth when dry. If made of paper, use a flannel, with a little sweet oil to rub on the spots, then rub with a dry cloth or old silk handkerchief.

Frozen potatoes will yield more starch, or flour, than fresh ones; it makes nice cake. Some families provide it simply for this purpose. Take a coarse tin grater, full of coarse holes, and grate a bushel or two; wash the pulp through a sieve over a tub; when you have done it in several waters until the starch is out, then let it settle in the tub and pour off the water. Repeat this, stirring it, well when a new water is added, until the water looks clear. It is then fit for use as starch or flour, after it is dried carefully.

Indian and rye meal should be stirred and kept in a cool place in summer, or they will become sour.

Save all your pieces of bread for puddings; dry them well or they will mould.

Examine your pickles, sweetmeats, and everything put away to keep, that nothing be lost for want of care.

If you buy your cheese, never get a large quantity at a time, especially in summer. Get your butter put up by some good family in the fall, for winter use, and in the summer engage it fresh every two weeks at least.

A hot shovel on a warming pan of coals, held over varnished furniture, will take out white spots. The place should be rubbed, while warm, with flannel.

Skim milk and water, with a bit of glue dissolved and hot, is good to restore rusty black Italian crape. It should be clapped and pulled dry, and it will look as well as new.

Bibbands of any color, should be washed in cold soapsuds and not rinsed. Iron them wet, and they will be stiff and nice as new, except some kinds of pink and blue, which will fade. These may be dyed to look as well as ever. Dip the blue in a little cold blue ink and water, and the pink in carmine, from a pink saucer, according to directions, and they will be perfectly restored.

Marble fire places should not be washed with suds, it will in time destroy the polish. After the dust is wiped off, rub the spots with a nice oiled cloth, then rub dry with a soft rag.

When you rub the knobs of your doors, use a piece of paste board as large as your two hands, with a small hole large enough to just encircle the knob in the center and a slit in the paper to let it in. This slipped on, will keep off all soil from the paint, and is a nice way of doing it.

If your flat irons are rough, or smoky, lay a little fine salt on a flat surface, and rub them well; it will prevent them from sticking to anything starched, and make them smooth.

Rub your griddle with fine salt, before you grease it, and your cakes will not stick. When walnuts have been kept until the meat is too much dried to be good, let them stand in milk and water eight hours, and dry them, and they will be fresh as when new.

It is a good plan to keep your different kinds of pieces, tape, thread, etc. in separate bags, and there is no time lost in looking for them.

The water in flower pots should be changed every day in summer, or it will become offensive and unhealthy, even if there is salt in them.

Hops should be picked when they are full grown and begin to be fragrant; by no means let them remain longer, as a strong wind or rain will injure them greatly. Spread them awhile to dry.

Oat straw is best for the filling of beds, and it is well to change it as often as once in a year.

Cedar chests are best to keep flannels and clothes, as moths never are found in them. Red cedar chips are good to keep in drawers, wardrobes, closets, trunks, etc. to keep out moths.

When clothes have acquired an unpleasant odor by being from the air, charcoal, laid in the folds, will remove it soon.

If black dresses have stains upon them, boil a handful of fig leaves in a quart of water, and reduce it to a pint; a sponge dipped in this liquid and rubbed upon them will entirely remove stains from crape, bombazines, etc.

In laying up furs for summer, lay a tallow candle in or near them, and all danger of worms will be obviated.

If you wish to select a carpet for durability, always choose a small figure, as they are the best cloth and will do best service.

Silver-plated candle sticks should be cleaned by pouring boiling hot water on the tops to remove the grease; when wiped dry, use whiting, rubbing them until bright. It does not not injure plated ware at all. If sockets are too large for the candle, wind the end with a paper, but it should not be in sight. Always light them to burn off the cotton before setting them up, but leave them long enough to light with ease.

Charcoal should never be used in sleeping rooms, unless in a grate; it is very deleterious, and frequently destroys life. If used in a furnace, let it be where there is air. It is very hurtful in a close room.

Wrap a wet sheet or blanket around you if obliged to expose your person in time of fire.

If the clothes catch fire, smother it instantly; put on a blanket, cloak, shawl, anything near; if away from any articles of the kind, take the clothes from the skirts, and if around the shoulders, draw them over and hold them fast; if at the lower garments, sit upon them, any way to *smother it quickly.*

A bit of soap rubbed on the hinges of a door will prevent their creaking.

Scotch snuff put on the holes where crickets come out, will destroy them.

Wood ashes and common salt, wet with water, will stop the cracks of the stove, and prevent the smoke from penetrating.

The bed hangings and window drapery in nurseries and common rooms should be of those colors that are easiest to the eyes. Green should be the prevailing color. A damp mop, passed under a bed to wipe off the dust as often as once a week, will prevent the visits of the nightly foe.

Carpets should be shook often, but with care. It is a good plan to hang them on a line, and take a new broom and beat and sweep them, after they have been shook awhile. This brings out the dust from the threads.

Silver spoons should never be used in the kitchen, unless for preparing preserves.

If you wish to have your free-stone hearths dark, wash them with suds; oil is good to rub in occasionally, and it will not show spots. If you wish to have it look like new, get free-stone powder of the cutters, and rub on wet; when dry, rub it off.

Sour beer may be converted into good vinegar by putting into it a pint of molasses and water, and in two or three days after half into a pint of vinegar; in ten days it will be first rate vinegar.

Ox gall is good to set colors; one tablespoon in a gallon of water is sufficient. It should be used without soap, and stirred well into the water. If you wash it afterwards use sand, and do not rub soap on the cloth.

Attend to mending the clothes of a family at least once a week. Stockings must be attended to, the heels lined or run, and thin places and holes well darned.

In winter, set the handle of your pump high as possible at night. When the weather is most severe, throw a rug or blanket over it, or it will freeze.

Have a heavy stone on the top of your pork, and see that it is kept under the brine. It is a good place to keep fresh meat in the summer, to keep from spoiling. Always have a plenty of clean dish water, and put it on as soon as the meat is prepared, as an invariable rule. No good housekeeper will allow this rule to be broken.

Never use lye to clean tin, it will spoil it soon; make it clean with suds, and rub with whiting, and it will look well and last much longer.

Never lay knives in hot water it injures the handles and destroys the polish.

Keep your mustard-spoon clean and your salt-spoons out of the salt.

Keep the cruets of your castor clean, well filled, and a piece of green baize or flannel under them.

A gallon of strong lye put in a tub of water will make it soft as rain water. It is a good plan to provide this, when you have not a plenty of rain water for dishes, etc.

Keep mats at your door, and wash them often. Always have the steps and entrance to your house clean. Keep a house cloth and a carpet broom.

Never clean gilded frames; many, in doing this, have ruined them. Several coats of white varnish, is good to preserve them, or they may be covered.

It is said that the half of a cranberry bound on a corn will eradicate it in the course of a few nights.

If you dry pumpkin, stew it first, dry it down well, do up in small cakes, and dry in an oven a little warm.

Never sit chairs to hit the paper or paint on walls. It soon soils them, and injures the chairs.

Keep your brass bright, your windows clear, and your furniture dusted.

CHOICE OF MEATS

Beef. When it is young, it will have a fine smooth open grain, be a good red, and feel tender. The fat should be white, rather than yellow; when that is of a deep color, the meat is seldom good. When fed with oil cakes, it is usually so, and the flesh is flabby.

Pork. If the rind is tough and thick, it is old. A thin rind is always preferable. When fresh, the meat will be smooth and cool; if clammy, it is tainted.

Mutton. Choose this by its fine grain, good color, and white fat.

Lamb. If it has a green or yellow cast, it is stale.

Veal. The whitest is the most juicy, and therefore preferable.

Bacon. If the rind is thin, the fat firm and of a red color, the lean of a good color and adhering to the bone, it is good and not old.

Hams. Stick a sharp knife under the bone; if it comes out clean, with a pleasant smell, it is good; but if the knife is daubed, and has a bad scent, do not buy it,

CHOICE OF FOWLS

Turkeys. If young, the legs will be black and smooth, the eyes lively, and the feet pliable. If old, the eyes will be sunk and the feet dry.

Geese. If young, the bill will be yellow, and the feet limber. If old, the bill and feet will be red and dry.

Hens. If their comb and legs are rough, they are old; if smooth and limber, they are young. In winter, hens should be fed in part with potatoes, turnips, carrots, cabbage, etc. to supply the want of seeds and grass they obtain in summer; also lime and pebbles should be put within their reach. This treatment will cause them to lay in winter. Bones, eggshells, and soaked corn are good.

Wild and Tame Ducks. If young, they will be limberfooted; if fat, they will be hard and thick on the lower part of the body. A wild duck has red feet and is smaller than tame ones.

Partridges. If young, will have a black bill and yellow legs; if old, the bill will be white and the legs blue. Old fowls, tame and wild, may be told by their hard, rough, or dry feet.

Hares and Rabbits. If young, they will be white and stiff, the ears will tear like brown paper. If old, the flesh will be dark, the body limber, and the ears tough. A rabbit, if old, will be limber and flimsy; if young, white and stiff.

CHOICE OF FISH

Cod. The gills should be very red, the fish thick at the neck, the flesh white and firm, and the eyes fresh. When flabby, they are not good.

Salmon. If new, the flesh is of a fine red, the gills particularly, the scales bright, and the whole fish stiff.

Shad. If good, are white and thick, gills red, and eyes bright, the fish stiff and firm. Season: April and May.

Mackerel. Their season is May, June, and July. They are so tender they do not carry or keep as well as other fish unsalted.

Striped Bass. If the eyes are sunken and gills pale, they have been from the water too long. Their fineness depends upon their being cooked immediately after they are killed.

Trout. These should be killed and dressed as soon as caught. When you buy them, see that the gills are red and hard to open, the eyes bright, and the body stiff. The season: July, August, and September.

Flounders soon become flabby and bad; they should be thick and firm, the eyes bright.

Lobsters, if they have not been too long taken, the claws will have a strong motion if you press your finger on the eyes. The heaviest are the best. The male, though generally smaller, has the highest flavor, the firmest flesh, and the deepest red. It may be known from the female by having a narrower tail.

Crabs. Those of middling size are the sweetest. The heaviest are best. When in perfection, the joints of the legs are stiff, and the body has an agreeable smell. The eyes look loose and dead when stale.

All fish should be well dressed and clean. Nothing is more unpalatable than fresh fish not thoroughly cooked.

Fresh Fish, when boiled, should be placed in cold, and shell fish in boiling water.

Fish should be garnished with horseradish or hard boiled eggs cut in rings and laid around the dish, or pastry, and served with no other vegetable but potatoes. This, or soup, is generally eaten at the commencement of a dinner.

TO KEEP OYSTERS

After washing them, lay them in a tub, with the deep part of the shell undermost, sprinkle them with salt and Indian meal or flour, fill the tub with cold water, and set in a cool place. Change the water daily, and they will keep fresh a fortnight.

RULES AND SUGGESTIONS

If meat or fish has acquired a slight unpleasant flavor, or does not smell perfectly fresh when prepared to boil, add a teaspoon of saleratus, and, unless it is bad, it will remove everything unpleasant in taste and smell. If the brine of meat or fish begins to have an unpleasant smell, scald and skim it, adding to it a spoonful or two of saleratus, pepper, and cinnamon, or throw it away and make new with the above ingredients.

Baking meats is easily done, and is a nice way of dressing a dinner, but a lean thin piece should never be used in this manner; it will all shrivel away.

The most economical way of cooking fresh meat is to boil it, if the liquid is used, as it always may be, for soups or broths.

It takes fat meat longer to bake than lean meat. All fresh meat should be kept awhile to make it tender.

In baking any kind of meats or puddings, if a stove is used, they will bear more fire at first than when they are nearly done.

In cooking by a fireplace, cooks impose on themselves discomfort, and incur a great waste in fuel, by making too much fire. Often, in summer, a fire is made like a small furnace to boil a pot. Three small sticks of wood or two with chips are sufficient at a time, if the pot or kettle is hung low, and but little inconvenience is felt from the fire. If you use a tin baker, the upper part or lid is sufficient to bake meats of almost any kind, if bright. Mutton, veal, pork, beef, etc. have been well cooked in this simple way. Set the dripping pan on a few coals with a small quantity of water, with merely the cover over it, and it will be done in the same time with less fire, less trouble, and no drawing out of smoke. Puddings may be done in the same way, and also custards.

When a pig is baked, it has a nice crisp to rub it over well with butter. It is better than oil, on account of the salt.

FOR CURING BEEF

Let your meat be cold, not frozen. For two hundred pounds use two quarts of molasses, half a pound of saltpeter, half a bushel of salt. Dissolve your saltpeter in warm water, then add your molasses, pack down your beef light; putting salt in your barrel and between each layer, let a suitable proportion be put between each layer of the above composition, until it is altogether. Use four or five quarts of salt to make a brine to cover the beef. Add two ounces of pearlash to the composition, and some think black pepper or cinnamon a great improvement. It will be very sweet, tender, and nice, either way.

TO KEEP HAMS IN SUMMER

Take them early in spring, and pack them in barrels with oats, barley, bran, or anything of the like, to protect them from flies, etc., and they will keep good. Another sure way is to rub the hams with pulverized niter; let them remain in the cellar three days, smoke a barrel three days, and make a pickle of salt and sugar, put in your hams and the work is done for the year.

PRESERVING POULTRY

No poultry should be kept longer than three years. The Poland topknots are considered the best for laying, and are the most hardy. They should be kept in winter where it is warm, have plenty of food and water, a box of gravel and lime to wallow in, and to pick from; some fresh meat when they cannot get insects; the scraps from tallow factories are good, and you will have no lack of fresh eggs.

REGULATION IN TIME OF COOKING

BOILING

The first caution is that whatever is used for boiling must be perfectly clean. The second, keep it constantly boiling. Salt meat may be put into cold water, while fresh meat should be put into hot water.

If a scum rises upon the surface, it must be skimmed off or it will discolor the meat. Never crowd the pot with meat, but leave room for plenty of water. Allow a quarter of an hour for every pound of meat. An old fowl will need boiling three or four hours. A full grown one an hour and a half. A pullet nearly an hour. A chicken about half an hour.

ROASTING

Beef. A large roasting piece will bake in four hours, a smaller one in three or three and a half.

Mutton. A leg, or saddle, will require two hours and a half each. A shoulder, loin, neck, and heart will each need an hour and a half or three quarters.

Veal. A fillet, which is the thick part of the hind quarter, will require four or five hours. A loin, or shoulder, from three to three and a half. A neck, or breast, nearly two hours.

Lamb. A hind-quarter of lamb is generally cooked whole, and requires nearly two hours. A fore-quarter, two hours. A leg nearly an hour and a half. A shoulder and breast, one hour.

Pork. A leg will require nearly three hours. A thick spare rib, two hours or more; a thin one, an hour and a quarter or half. A loin will bake in two hours or more. A pig, three or four weeks old, will require but about an hour and a half.

Venison. A large haunch will require four hours and a half; a smaller one, about three hours.

POULTRY

Turkey. The largest size will require three hours; a smaller one, two hours; the least size, an hour and a half.

Goose. A full grown goose will require nearly two hours; but a young one will roast in an hour.

Duck. The largest will bake in less than an hour ; the smaller ones in half an hour. Pricking with a fork will tell you whether done or not. Fowls should be well done through, and all meats but beef; this is generally preferred rare done.

WHEN HANDLING FISH, SOUPS, MEATS, ETC.

BAKED SHAD

In the first place make a stuffing of the head and cold boiled ham, seasoned with pepper, salt, cloves, and sweet majoram; moisten it with beaten yolk of an egg. Stuff the fish and the outside with the yolk of egg and some of the stuffing. Lay the fish in a deep pan, putting its tail to its mouth. Pour in the pan a little water, and put in a piece of butter rolled in flour. Bake two hours, pour the gravy round it, garnish with lemon sliced, and send to table. Any fish may be baked in this way.

TO BOIL SHAD AND OTHER FISH

Split, wash, and dry in a cloth. Season with salt and pepper. Grease the gridiron, lay the outside uppermost of the fish over coals, and broil a quarter of an hour or more. Butter it well, season with pepper and salt, and send to table hot.

STURGEON CUTLETS OR STEAKS

Take off the skin, cut from the tail-piece slices half an inch thick, rub them with salt, and broil over a hot fire. Butter and sprinkle on Cayenne pepper. Or first dip them in beaten yolk of egg and bread crumbs, and wrap them up in buttered papers, and broil over a clear fire. Send to the table without the papers.

TO BOIL FRESH SALMON

Scale and clean, cutting open no more than is necessary. Place it in a kettle of cold water, with a handful of salt. Let it boil slowly, but it should be well cooked, about a quarter of an hour to a pound of fish. Skim it well, and as soon as done, lift it carefully into a napkin to absorb the moisture, and wrap it close. Send to table on a hot dish, garnish with horseradish and curled parsely or boiled eggs cut in rings, laid round the dish. Oyster sauce is best with fresh boiled fish.

SMOKED SALMON

Clean and scale, cut the fish up the back, and take out the roe and the bone neatly. Rub inside and out, with equal parts of Havana sugar; add salt and a little saltpeter. Press the fish flat with a board and put weights on it; leave for two days. Drain from the salt, wipe it, stretch it open, and fasten with a pin or stick. Then hang up, and smoke over a wood fire five or six days. When used, soak the slices in luke-warm water, and broil for breakfast.

LOBSTERS AND CRABS

Put them in boiling water with a handful of salt. Boil half an hour or an hour in proportion to its size. If boiled too long, the meat will be hard and stringy. When done, wipe dry, take off the shell, and take out the blue veins and what is called the lady-fingers, as they are unwholesome and not to be eaten. Send it to table cold with the body and tail split open and the claws taken off. Lay the large claws next the body, the small ones outside; garnish with double parsely.

TO DRESS LOBSTERS COLD

Take the fish out of the shell, divide it in small pieces, mash up the scarlet meat, and prepare a salad mixture of Cayenne pepper, salt, sweet oil, venegar, and mustard; mix the lobster with this preparation together and serve in a dish.

CLAMS

Wash them clean with a cloth and rinse them; put them in a cooking vessel with a small quantity of water and boil them until the shells open, then take

out the clams and remove the shells. Cook them in the same water, adding salt, pepper, and a good quantity of butter. Roll crackers, and when done stir them in. Toast a few slices of bread to lay in the tureen and pour over the clams. Send to the table hot.

CLAM CRIDDLES

Make a wheat batter in the usual way, chop the clams fine, and stir in. Bake in the common way. A nice breakfast dish.

TO FRY OYSTERS

Make a batter, wipe the oysters dry, dip them in the batter, roll them in crumbs of bread and mace, finely powdered, and fry in butter.

OYSTER PATTIES

Stew some large oysters with a little nutmeg, a few cloves, some yolk of egg boiled hard and grated, a little butter, and as much of the oyster liquor as will cover them; when stewed a few moments, take them out of the pan to cool. Have shells of puff paste previously baked in small patty pans, and lay two or three oysters in each.

CODFISH CAKES

Soak codfish over night and scald it; add to it twice its quantity of boiled potatoes, knead all well together, make in small cakes, and fry in butter. If, after having boiled codfish, you have some left, use it in the same way. It makes a nice and wholesome dish.

FOR BROILING CHICKENS

Separate the breast from the back, beat them flat, as you would steak, and lay the under side to the fire until it is above half done. Cover them over with a square tin or other convenient covering, and they will be done through much sooner. Great care should be taken not to let the flesh side burn, but they should be of a fine brown color. When the different parts of the chicken are done, turn turn some melted butter over them, with a little salt and pepper.

TO BROIL A STEAK

Pound it well, striking it with the edge to cut the fibres, when sufficiently thin and tender, lay it upon the gridiron, and cook it over hot coals, turning it often; when the blood settles upon the top, hold the platter near, and take it carefully on that it may not be lost; let the steak lie upon the platter until everything is in readiness, though not over a minute, then lay it back on a few fresh coals until done. Have butter melted, and, when the steak is on the platter, pepper and salt it, pour over the butter, and take it on hot. The meat should not be pressed to obtain the blood, it makes the meat dry and greatly impairs its richness. It should not be commenced until everything is ready. It requires constant attention.

TO FRY HAM

Cut a ham through the middle, so that you get the fat and lean in good proportions; lay it in your pan or spider, and cover it that it may cook tender in the steam. When nearly done, let it finish open that the steam may evaporate, and that it may slightly brown.

TO ROAST PORK

When you roast that which has the skin on, take a sharp knife, and cut it through the rind, that it may crisp well. If a leg, cut a hole under the twist, and stuff it with chopped bread, seasoned with pepper, salt, and sage, and skewer it up. Roast it crisp and handsomely brown. Make a drawn gravy of the dripping and serve it with apple-sauce. This is called mock-goose. The spare-rib should be sprinkled with flour, pepper, and a little salt, and turned often until nearly done; then let the round side lie up until nicely brown. Make the gravy of the dripping, prepared with flour, and seasoned well with salt. Never send it to the table without apple-sauce, salad, pickles, or slaw. Pork must be well done. To every pound allow a quarter of an hour. For example, twelve pounds will require three hours. If it be a thin piece of that weight, two hours will roast it.

TO ROAST VEAL

If the leg is used, it may be stuffed like pork, and requires nearly as much time to bake. It should be done a fine brown, and often basted.

TO ROAST BEEF

Never salt fresh beef before you cook it in any way, for it draws out the gravy, and leaves the meat dry. If the roasting-piece is large, bake it three hours, otherwise two and a half. Make your gravy of the dripping.

TO ROAST A PIG

When well dressed and washed, prepare a stuffing of chopped bread, seasoned well with pepper, salt, sage, and butter, soaked enough to make it soft. Fill the body, and sew it up with strong thread. Flour it well all over, and when the oven is well heated through, put it on dripping pans that will catch all the gravy. Let it stand in two or three hours, according to the size of the pig. Let it be well crisped, and of course handsomely brown. When you take it from the oven, mash two spoonsful of flour, with butter enough to mix well, and dip on the dripping a little at a time at first until melted; then pour it on, stirring it until thickened, season it well with salt, and add to it the brains bruised fine, and then send it to the table. The head must be cut off, and laid upon the platter.

TO ROAST GEESE AND DUCKS

See to it that they are well dressed, and then boil them an hour or more, according to their age. When they begin to feel tender take them out, and having your stuffing prepared of bread, salt, pepper, and butter—some like sage—made soft, fill the body, and fasten it up with thread. Roast them brown. Make your gravy of the dripping; serve both with apple-sauce. Poultry, when roasted or boiled, should have the wings and legs fastened close to the body, with a cord tied around.

TO ROAST A TURKEY

Prepare the stuffing with bread, salt, pepper, butter, cinnamon, or nutmeg, or a little lemon peel, or parsley and thyme; chop and mix all well together with one or two eggs beat well. With this dressing stuff the body and the breast, and sew them with a strong thread. Roast the turkey of a fine brown, not burning it. It will be well done in one hour and a half, or, if old and very large, two hours or more. Make a gravy of drawn butter and the dripping. Another sauce is made of half a pint of oysters boiled in a pan, thickened with a lump of butter rolled in flour. Only let it boil once. Serve this by itself, in connection with other gravy, for every person does not like oyster sauce.

TO ROAST SNIPES OR WOODCOCKS

Flour and baste them until done. Have ready a dice or two of bread, toasted and dipped in the dripping, to lay on the dish. Lay them on the toast. Make a gravy of butter and flour mashed, with the dripping poured on and stirred until scalded.

TO BOIL A DUCK OR RABBIT

Use a good deal of water, and skim it as often as anything rises. Half an hour will boil them. Make a gravy of sweet cream, butter, and flour, a little parsley chopped small, pepper, and salt, and stew until done; lay them in a dish and pour the gravy over them.

TO BOIL A TONGUE

Put a tongue into a pot over night and soak, until three hours before dinner, then boil until noon.

TO BOIL A LEG OF LAMB, MUTTON, OR VEAL

Let the water boil before any fresh meat is put in, that the richness of the meat may not be lost. Boil a piece of pork with either of the above, but not with vegetables; when done, make a gravy with drawn butter.

MUTTON CHOPS

Take pieces of mutton that are not good for steak, rib, or other pieces, have them cut small, and boil them in water sufficient to cook them tender; add salt, pepper, and, if not fat enough to make good gravy, a little butter; or, if preferred, cut a little pork fine and boil with the meat, which will make it nearly salt enough, and sufficient gravy; let them fry, after the water is out, a little brown.

FRICASSEED BEEF

Take any piece of beef from the fore-quarter, such as is generally used for corning, and cook it tender in just enough water to have it all evaporate in cooking. When about half done, put in salt enough to just season it well, and half a teaspoon of pepper. If the water should not be done out soon enough, turn it off and let it fry fifteen minutes, turning it often; and it is even better than the best roast beef. Make your gravy of the dripping. Take one or two tablespoons of flour, and add first the fat; when mixed, pour on the hot juice of the meat or hot water from the teakettle, and your gravy will be nice. Serve with vegetables and salad, or apple-sauce.

VEAL CUTLET

Cut your veal as if for steak or frying, put clean nice lard or butter in your pan, and let it be hot. Beat up an egg on a plate and have flour on another; dip the pieces first in the egg, then in the flour on both sides, and lay in the pan and fry until done, turning it carefully once. This makes an excellent dish, if well prepared. This way is superior to batter.

TO FRY PORK

If too salty, freshen by heating it in water after it is cut in slices. Then pour off the water and fry until done. Take out the pork, and stir a spoonful of flour into the lard, and turn in milk or cream enough to thicken. This makes a more delicate gravy, and is very palatable.

TO FRICASSEE A CHICKEN

Cut it in pieces, jointing it well, and boil it tender with a slice or two of pork cut fine. When nearly done, add half a teaspoon of pepper and salt to just season it. When tender, turn off the water and add half a pound of butter or nearly that, and let it fry a while. Then take out the chicken, and stir in two or three spoonsful of flour previously dissolved in cold water, and add the water from the chicken. Let it boil, and pour it upon the chicken on the platter. This makes a superior dish, and needs no vegetables but mashed potatoes.

HAM SANDWICHES

Slightly spread thin slices of bread; if you choose, spread on a very little mustard. Lay very thin slices of boiled ham between; tongue, sliced or grated, may be used instead. Lay them on plates, to be used at suppers.

HEAD-CHEESE

Take the heads, tongues, and feet, and other pieces if you choose. Make them clean and soak them. Then boil until they will slip from the bones easily. Chop and season with salt, black pepper, cloves, sage, or sweet marjoram rubbed fine. Mix well and place it in a pan; set a plate on the top with a weight upon it. In two days it will be cold and fit for use. Turn it out and cut it in slices for tea or suppers.

MOCK DUCK

Take a steak about as large as a breakfast plate, beat it out, fill it with a bread stuffing prepared as for a turkey, and sew it up. Fry one hour in the dripping from roast beef or butter. Turn it and keep it covered until near done. When you take it up, turn in half a cup of hot water in the gravy that has been previously seasoned and pour over. It will be thickened with the stuffing that falls from it.

RICE BALLS

Take the waste pieces of steak, or baked meat, chop fine, and season with salt, pepper, cloves, or cinnamon. Wash rice and mix with it, then tie up in cloths to shape balls; boil half an hour and serve with drawn butter.

FRENCH ROLLS

Cut strips of beefsteak to make a roll as long as a knife blade and larger than a sausage, stuff with a prepared stuffing, and sew up and bake, or fry in batter. Melt butter for a gravy.

CHICKENS BOILED

The wings and legs of fowls should be fastened to the body by a cord tied around to keep them in place, instead of skewers. When thus prepared, let them lie in skim milk two hours. Then put them in cold water, cover them, and boil over a slow fire. Skim the water clean. Serve with white sauce or drawn butter.

BOUILLI

Boil seven or eight pounds of beef in more water than enough to cover it. Remove the scum as it rises, then put in two carrots, two turnips, two onions, two heads of celery, two or three cloves, a faggot of parsley, and sweet herbs. Let it boil gently four or five hours. Put a carrot, a turnip, an onion, and a head of celery in to cook whole, take them out when done, and cut in small squares. Take out the meat carefully, skim off the fat, and lay the sliced vegetables into the soup; add a spoonful of ketchup to heighten the flavor. Pour in a soup tureen and serve as other soup.

MOCK TURTLE SOUP

Boil a calf's bead, a knuckle of veal, and a piece of ham six or eight hours. Reserve a part of the veal for force meat balls to be added. Skim it carefully, and when the scum ceases to rise, season with salt, pepper, cloves, and mace; add onions and sweet herbs and six sliced potatoes; stew gently half an hour. Just before you take it up, add a half pint of white wine. Make balls about the size of half an egg, boil part, and fry the remainder; put in a dish by themselves. For these take lean veal, pork, and brains, chop fine, and season with salt, pepper, or cloves, mace, sweet herbs, curry powder, with the yolk of an egg to hold it together.

MACARONI SOUP

Make a nice veal soup, seasoned with sweet marjoram, parsley, salt, pepper, mace, and two or three onions. Break in small pieces a quarter of a pound of macaroni, and simmer in milk and water till swelled and tender. Strain and add to the soup. To the milk, add half a pint of cream; thicken it with two spoonsful of flour, and stir gradually into the soup, and boil a few moments before serving.

VERMICELLI SOUP

Make a rich soup of veal, mutton, or fowls—old fowls that are not good for other purposes will do for soup. A few slices of ham will be an addition. Season with salt, butter, two onions sliced, sweet herbs, and a head of selery cut small. Boil until the meat falls to pieces. Strain it and add a quarter of a pound of vermicelli that has been scalded in boiling water. Season to your taste with salt and Cayenne pepper, and let it boil five minutes. Lay two slices of bread in your tureen and pour the soup upon it.

TO BOIL A HAM

Soak, according to its age, twelve or twenty-four hours. Have it more than covered with cold water, let it simmer two or three hours, and then boil an hour and a half or two hours; skim it carefully. When done, take it up and skin it neatly; dress it with cloves and spots of pepper laid on accurately. You may cut writing or tissue paper in fringe and twist around the shank bone if you like. It should be cut past the center, nearest the hock, in very thin slices.

FINE SAUSAGES

Have two-thirds lean and one-third fat pork, chop very fine. Season with nine teaspoons of pepper, nine of salt, and three of powdered sage to every pound of meat. Add half a cup of sugar to every pan full. Warm the meat, that you can mix it well with your hands; do up a part in small patties, with a little flour mixed with them, and the rest pack in jars. When used, do it up in small cakes and flour on the outside, and fry in butter or alone. They should not be covered or they will fall to pieces. A little cinnamon to a part of them will be a pleasant addition; the sugar is a great improvement. They should be kept where it is cool but not damp. They are very nice for breakfast.

TO BROIL HAM

Cut the pieces in thin slices; soak them in hot water fifteen or twenty minutes. Dry them in a cloth, lay them on a hot gridiron, and broil a few moments. Butter and season with a little pepper. Cold boiled ham is better to broil than raw, and will require no soaking. If you wish to serve fried eggs with it, do it according to the directions: lay one on each slice of ham and send it to the table hot.

PORK STEAK

This should be broiled the same as beef, except it requires to be done slower and much longer. If there is too much fire, it will blaze. Cut in around the bone that there shall be nothing that has a raw appearance. Season with butter, salt, and pepper. They may be cooked in cutlets like veal, with a little powdered sage and hard crumbs or flour or fried in butter.

A PORK STEW

Take pieces of fresh pork, sweet bread, liver, heart, tongue, and skirts. Boil in just water enough to cook them tender. Before they are done, season them with salt and considerable pepper, and let them fry after the water is out to a fine brown. It is an excellent dish.

TO ROAST A BEEF'S HEART

Cut open, to remove the ventricles or pipes, soak in water to free it of blood, and parboil it about ten minutes. Prepare a highly seasoned stuffing and fill it. Tie a string around to secure it. Roast till tender. Add butter and flour to the gravy, and serve it up hot in a covered dish. Garnish it with cloves stuck in over it, and eat with jelly. They are good boiled tender and fried in butter, cut in thin slices, seasoned with salt and pepper.

BEEF CAKES

Chop pieces of roast beef very fine. Mix grated bread crumbs, chopped onions, and parsley; season with pepper and salt; moisten with a little of the dripping or ketchup; cold ham or tongue may be added to improve it. Make in broad flat cakes, and spread a coat of mashed potatoes on the top and bottom of each. Lay a

piece of butter on every cake and set in an oven to brown. Other cold meats may be prepared in the same way for a breakfast dish. Slices of cold roast beef may be broiled, seasoned with salt and pepper, and well buttered; served hot. They may be chopped fine, seasoned well, warmed with a little butter, dripping, or water, seasoned well with salt and pepper, and laid upon a moist toast for a breakfast dish.

TO FRY CALVES' LIVER

Cut the liver in thin slices, season with pepper, salt, and, if you like, sweet herbs and parsley. Dredge with flour, and fry brown in lard or drippings. Cook it well, and serve with its own gravy. A calf's heart may be dressed in this manner. Slices of cold boiled ham may be added as an improvement.

PEA SOUP

If you use dry peas, soak them over night in a warm place. Early next morning boil them an hour, adding a teaspoon of saleratus ten minutes before you change the water. Then, with fresh water and a pound of salt pork, boil three or four hours, or until they are perfectly soft. Green peas require only about an hour.

TO STEW BEEF

Take a good piece of fresh beef, not too fat, rub with salt, and boil in water just enough to cover it. An hour before you take it up, add pared potatoes and parsnips, if you have them, split. Let them cook till tender, and turn the meat several times. Serve them up together with gravy. The water should be cooked out, which will leave the vegetables a light brown. Sweet potatoes are good cooked in this way.

BOLOGNA SAUSAGES

Boil fresh beef, chop it fine, and season it with Cayenne and black pepper and cloves; put it in cloth bags, and cut off for tea.

FRESH MEAT BALLS

Boil the liver, heart, tongue, etc.; chop and season with drawn butter.

TO MAKE SAUSAGES IN SUMMER

Chop raw pork and veal fine, and season with salt, pepper, and sage; add a little flour, and do up in balls to fry, and they make a fine fresh dish, equal to those made entirely of pork.

FRESH MEAT GRIDDLES

Chop all the bits of cold fresh beef or veal, season with salt and pepper; make a griddle batter, and lay on a spoonful on the iron well buttered, to prevent its sticking. Then add a spoonful of the chopped meat, then a spoonful of batter over the meat. When cooked on one side, turn it, and when done, carry them on hot, and they are very nice.

A BEEF OR VEAL PIE

Take the cold pieces after baking, and make a light crust, like tea-biscuit, only a little shorter. Lay the the crust around the dish, not on the bottom. Then season your meat with salt and pepper, and butter between each layer; add water to make it moist with gravy, then lay on the cover, and bake three-quarters of an hour. It makes a fine dish occasionally.

TO MAKE A POT-PIE

Make your sponge as you would for biscuit, only shorter; when you do it up let it get just light, putting into the batter a little saleratus and salt; when light take it on to the board, and cut it in pieces like biscuit, only let them lie and rise without kneading them at all. When the meat is tender there should be enough water to come just over the meat. Season it well with salt and pepper, dissolve flour in cold water, and stir in enough to thicken it well. If the meat is very lean put in butter, and when boiling hot lay the crust in over the surface and shut it up close. Do not allow it to be opened again in half an hour, when it will be ready for the table, as light and nice as sponge.

TO MAKE A SOUP

Beef soup should be stewed four hours at least, over a moderate fire, with a handful of rice and just water enough to keep it covered. An hour before it is done put in two or three common size onions, and ten or twelve common potatoes, pared and sliced, and a few carrots, if you like; at the same time put in salt to season it well, and half a teaspoon of pepper. A little lemon-peel some like, cut in thin slices; others prefer powdered sage and parsley, or cavory, two teaspoonsful. Stir up two or three eggs with milk and flour, and drop it in with a spoon. This makes a soup look nice; but bread broken into the tureen is preferable, with the soup taken over it. If you have other dishes, this should be the first for the table.

ALAMODE BEEF

Tie up a round of beef to keep in shape, make a stuffing of bread, as you would for a turkey, adding sweet herbs if you have them; cut holes in the beef, and put in half the stuffing. Tie the beef up in a cloth, just cover it with water, and let it boil an hour and a half or more; then turn the liquor off, and let the beef brown over a slow fire; turn it often. Then take it out and add a little water, and make the remainder of the stuffing in balls and lay them in, and when boiled they are ready to serve in a boat or to turn over the meat.

SOUSE

Boil it until it is tender and will slip off the bone. If designed to pickle, and keep on hand, throw it into cold water and take out the bones. Then pack it into a jar, and boil with the jelly liquor an equal quantity of vinegar; add salt enough to seasons and cloves, cinnamon, pepper enough to make it pleasant. Pour it on the souse scalding hot, and when wanted for use, warm it in the liquor, or make a batter and dip each piece in, and fry in hot butter. This way is usually preferred, and is as nice as tripe.

TRIPE

This should be boiled tender, pickled, and cooked like souse, or broiled like steak, buttered and peppered well. If not pickled, it should be kept in salt and water, and changed every day while it lasts.

CHICKEN PIE

Boil the chickens tender, or nearly so, having them cut in pieces. Make a rich crust, adding a little saleratus and an egg or two to make it light and puff. Lay it around the sides of the pan, and then lay in the chickens; between each layer sprinkle

in flour, pepper, salt, and butter, with a thin slice of paste here and there. Then add the water in which they were boiled, and cover them. They should be baked an hour or an hour and a half, according to the size of the pie.

TO COOK PIGEONS

After they are well dressed, put a slice of salt pork and a little ball of stuffing into the body of each. Flour the pigeons well, and lay them close in the bottom of the pot. Just cover them with water, throw in a piece of butter, and let them stew an hour and a quarter if young, if old stew longer. This is preferred to roasting or any other way they can be prepared. They may be cooked in the same way without stuffing.

TO COOK FRESH FISH OR EELS

The fish should not be laid in until the fat is hot. Beat up an egg or two, and with a pastry brush lay it on the fish, shake crumbs of bread and flour mixed over the fish, and fry them a light brown; turn them once, and take care they do not break. A more common method is to fry them after salt pork, dipping them in Indian meal or flour. Lay the skin uppermost, to prevent its breaking. Soaking fresh fish or fresh meat in water is injurious; after they are well dressed, they should be kept dry in a cool place and, if necessary, salted.

SOUNDS AND TONGUES

Make a batter of eggs and flour, or beat one egg, and dip them in the egg and then in the flour. Fry in butter, or boil them twenty minutes, and use drawn butter gravy.

TO BOIL FRESH CODFISH

Put it in when the water is boiling hot, and boil it twenty or thirty minutes, according to the size of the fish. Use melted butter or oyster sauce for gravy.

TO MAKE A CHOWDER

Lay four or five slices of salt pork in the bottom of the pot, let it cook slow that it may not burn; when done brown, take it out, and lay in fish cut in lengthwise slices. Then layer crackers, sliced onions, and very thin sliced potatoes, with some of the pork that was fried, and then add another layer of fish, and so on. Strew a little salt and pepper over each layer; over the whole pour a bowl full of flour and water well stirred up, enough to come up even with what you have in the pot. A sliced lemon adds to the flavor. A few clams improve it. Let it be so covered that the steam cannot escape. It must not be opened until cooked, to see if it is well seasoned.

TO BOIL SALT CODFISH

Lay it in water over night to soak. Then put it in water to cook, and when the water becomes scalding hot, let it remain in that scalding state two or three hours. There should be but little water used, and not boiled at all, that it may not grow hard.

CODFISH TOAST

Shred it in fine pieces, and soak it in cold water until sufficiently fresh, then drain it well, and stir into it a tablespoon of flour, half a teacup of sweet cream, two thirds of a teacup of milk, and one egg if convenient. Season it well with pepper, and let it scald slow, stirring it well. Make a nice moist toast, well seasoned, and lay it on the platter, with the fish over it. It is ready for the table and is a fine dish. Made as above, without toast, is also good; with vegetables, butter may be used instead of cream.

BUTTERED CODFISH

Shred it fine and soak as above; when the water is well drained, have a piece of butter as large as an egg, melted and hot. Stir into the fish a spoonful of flour to absorb all the water, and then lay it into the hot butter, stirring it well about five minutes; then lay it upon the platter, pepper, and send it up. Some prefer this to any other mode of preparation.

STEWED OYSTERS

They should be only boiled a few minutes. Add to them a little water, salt, and a sufficient quantity of butter and pepper; roll crackers fine and stir in. Some prefer toast of nice bread laid in the bottom of the dish, with less cracker. Either are nice. They should be served hot.

CURRY SPICES

CURRY-POWDER

Six ounces of pale-colored turmeric, five ounces of black pepper, thirteen ounces of coriander seed, three ounces of cummin seed, two ounces of fenugreek seed, one ounce of Cayenne pepper. All these ingredients are to be ground fine separately and well mixed.

TO MAKE CURRY

Take a fowl, or any white meat, and cut it up in joints or small pieces. Fry them in a little butter until they are light brown and put them on a plate. Have ready three medium-sized onions cut fine, and fry them also; then add a tablespoon and a half of

the curry-powder and two of flour. Mix it smooth, and moisten with a pint of weak broth or water; peel and core a good-sized apple, cut it in small pieces, and add to the sauce; put the meat in and let it stew gently for an hour. Before serving, skim very carefully and strain the sauce. Plain boiled rice should be served with it.

EGGS

EGGS OF A HEN

Those that approach nearest to roundness produce females, while those that are more pointed produce males.

PRESERVATION

Put a layer of salt in the bottom of a jar, and stick the eggs point downwards into the salt to make a layer. Then add another layer of salt, and then of eggs, until the jar is full. This keeps them fresh and good. They may be kept well in lime water and salt. They should be well covered, and kept in a cool place. One cracked one will spoil the whole. They are cheapest in spring and during September. If you have hens of your own, keep a jar of lime water always ready, and put in the eggs as they are brought from the nest. Jars that hold four or six quarts are best; it is well to renew the lime water occasionally. There is no sure way of discerning the freshness of eggs. It is always best to break them separately in a saucer when used. If you get them to pack, lay them in a pan of water, and those that float will not answer to put away.

TO BOIL EGGS

The fresher they are, the longer time they require. Three minutes will boil them very soft, five minutes will cook hard all but the yolk, and eight minutes will cook them hard through. Ten minutes will cook them hard enough for dressing to fish or salad. If you boil them in a tin egg boiler placed on the table, scalded well, it will take five minutes just to boil them soft. The most convenient way to eat a boiled egg, is from an egg-cup. Use salt, butter, and pepper.

TO FRY EGGS

This is done after frying ham usually. If there is not enough gravy from the meat, add some clean lard, and have it hot. Break the eggs into a bowl, and slip them carefully in the lard without breaking the yolk. Let them fry gradually, dipping the hot lard over them until they are cooked sufficiently without turning them at all. Then lay them on a plate or dish as they were cooked, and they look much more delicate than if they had been turned.

POACHED EGGS

The beauty of eggs cooked in this way is to have the yolk blushing through the white; which should be just hardened to form a transparent veil for the egg. Have some boiling water in a stewpan, let it be half full, break each egg separately into a saucer, and carefully slip it into the water. When the eggs are set, put it on the coals, and as soon as the water boils, they are done.

SCRAMBLED EGGS

Beat seven or eight eggs quite lightly and throw them in a pan with salt and butter. Stir them until well thickened, and turn them on a hot dish, without allowing any to adhere to the pan. This is excellent with a light breakfast.

OMELET

Five or six eggs will make a good sized omelet; break them into a basin, and beat them well with a fork. Add a salt-spoon of salt, some chopped parsley, and two ounces of butter. Have the same amount of butter hot in the pan and stir in the omelet until it begins to set. Turn it up all round the edges, and when it is a nice brown, it is done. Turn a plate up over it and take it up by turning the pan upside down. Serve hot. It should never be done until just wanted.

PICKLED EGGS

Boil twelve eggs quite hard, and lay them in cold water to peel off the shell. Then put them in a stone jar with a quarter of a pound of mace, the same of cloves, a sliced nutmeg, a tablespoon of whole pepper, a little ginger root, and a peach-leaf. Fill the jar with boiling vinegar and cover it that it may cool slowly. After three days, boil the vinegar again, and return it to the eggs and spices. They will be fit for use in a fortnight.

BREAD OMELET

Put a handful of bread crumbs in a sauce pan, a little cream, salt, pepper, and nutmeg. When the bread has absorbed all the cream, then break into it ten eggs, beat all together and fry like an omelet.

WHEN MAKING CHEESE

Take new milk, heat it ninety degrees or more than blood warm. Have your rennet previously made, in proportions of a quart of water to a piece of rennet as big as your hand. Put in enough to turn it. If the milk is too hot, it will be tough; and if there is too much rennet, it will be strong.

The milk after it is warmed should be placed in a tub kept for the purpose. When the curd has set, take a long knife and cut through the curd both ways carefully, and do not break it until the whey is seen to separate. Then let it remain until the whey covers the curd well. Then place a ladder over another tub with a strainer and basket, and dip the curd and whey carefully into the strainer; let it lie and drain until it has nearly ceased, and then move it by raising the sides of the strainer. It should not be urged, as that will press out the cream and alter the taste of the cheese. If prepared the same day, the curd must be salted enough to taste right, and then put in a hoop, strainer, and all, made smooth as possible, with a cover that will just fit inside, and placed in a press. When turned, which should be done in two hours, put it in a cheese cloth wet with salt and water, and in eight or nine hours turn again and pare the edges. Let it remain twelve or fourteen hours, then take it out and oil with salt butter, and place it where it will have air but not be exposed to flies.

NEW METHOD

It is said that those who have but a small quantity of milk, after making it as above described, may, after pressing out the whey as well as possible with the hands, press it compactly in an earthen or stone jar and cover it over with several folds of dry linen or cotton cloth. When this is saturated, remove it and place a dry one in its stead. It will be as clear of whey as if pressed, and the next day add another curd, pursuing the same process until full. This makes cheese solid, and free from moisture as the press. The labor is much less, and the care of it comparatively nothing.

CHEESE MADE FROM POTATOES

Cheese, it is said, of an extremely fine quality, is manufactured from potatoes in Thuringia and part of Saxony, in the following manner: After having collected a quantity of potatoes of a good quality, giving the preference to the large white kind, they are boiled in a cauldron, and, becoming cold, they are peeled and reduced to pulp, either by means of a grater or a mortar. To five pounds of this pulp, which ought to be as equal as possible, is added one pound of sour milk and the necessary quantity of salt. The whole is kneaded together, and the mixture covered up and allowed to remain for three or four days, according to the season. At the end of this time, it is kneaded again, and the cheese placed in little baskets, where the superfluous moisture is allowed to escape. They are then allowed to dry in the shade, and placed in layers in large pots or vessels, where they must remain for fifteen days. The older these cheeses are the more their quality improves. Two kinds of them are made. The first, which is the most common, is made according to the proportions above indicated; the second is made with four parts of potatoes and four parts of ewe or cow milk. These cheeses have this advantage over every other kind, that they do not engender worms, and keep fresh for a great number of years, provided they are placed in a dry situation and in well closed vessels.

DUTCH CHEESE

Take your milk in summer, after it is skimmed and thick, put it in a kettle, and hang it over the fire until scalded and the curd has settled to the bottom but not to boil. Strain it out and separate it from the whey, then turn it in a pan and add salt, sweet cream, or butter, and do up in small balls for tea. They are best when fresh made.

CHAPTER 5: USEFUL NOTIONS ON VEGETABLES

POTATOES

They should be kept covered in winter to keep them from freezing, but in summer they need a dry place, and should have the sprouts rubbed off. When boiled, they should be washed and only pared where it is necessary. If they are inclined to crack, put them in cold water. When they are done, pour it off, and keep them covered by the fire until they are wanted for the table. Old potatoes will require an hour if large; new ones, half an hour. Never send them to the table with the skins on, unless they are new. Potatoes are nice baked, but they require more than an hour in cooking.

When the skins become shrivelled in spring, they should be pared, sliced, and boiled in a small quantity of water, as they will require but about fifteen minutes in boiling. Mash them with a beetle for the purpose, season them well with salt, sweet cream, or milk, enough to moisten, or butter will answer the same purpose. Dish them, and if you prefer, brown them on the top. Cold ones may be cooked in various ways. They are very nice sliced thin as possible and warmed carefully in half a teacup of cream, or milk, and salt to season them well. They make a favorite dish by being sliced rather thick, broiled on a gridiron, and served with butter and salt. They are nice and look well grated, minced with the yolk of an egg, made in small cakes, and fried in butter for breakfast. "Snow balls" are mealy potatoes boiled, peeled, and pressed in a cloth into the shape of a ball. Potatoes boiled and mashed while hot are good to use in making bread, cake, puddings, etc.; they save flour and less shortening is necessary.

SWEET POTATOES

Should be kept in earth or sand in cold weather, or they will be scarcely eatable after October. The best way to cook them, is to bake them. They may be peeled and boiled as other potatoes. They are also good stewed with fresh pork, veal, or beef, or they may be half boiled, peeled, sliced, and fried in butter or nice dripping.

WINTER SQUASH

This is a very nice vegetable. It is good to use in August, when it should be stored in a dry place, and it in winter, when it should be stored in a warm place. Pare it, scrape out the seeds, cut it in pieces, boil it in a small quantity of water, or if you are boiling potatoes, lay it on the top and cover it, that it may cook well. When done, which will be in half or three quarters of an hour, press out the water as dry as possible, mash well, and season with salt and butter.

SUMMER SQUASH

They are good when yellow and tender, but when the skin becomes hard they are out of season. Cut off the top and lower part, wash and boil with other vegetables or alone as long as potatoes. If they are large and not very tender, boil them longer. Have a cloth strainer ready in a pan, and put them into it when done; if the seeds are large, take them out, but if not, let them remain; press the squash by winding to the ends of the strainer, and use a beetle to extract all the water; then lay it in the pan along, add salt and butter, mash well, and it will be a nice dish indeed. Cooked in any other way, they will be watery and insipid.

TURNIPS

Pare or scrape the outside; if large, cut them in half or quarters; boil as long as potatoes. When tender, take them in a pan, lay a small plate over them to press out the water; when pressed once, heap them high and press again, repeating it until the water is out. Then add salt and butter and send them to the table hot. Dish them, and lay the pepper in regular spots if you wish to have it look well. Turnips should be kept in the cellar, where they will not dry or freeze. When cooked with boiled salted meats, they are best sent to the table whole.

PARSNIPS

Pare or scrape or split them in two, that the inside may cook tender, which will be in two or three hours, according to their size. Dry them in a cloth when done, and pour melted butter over them in a dish, or serve plain. They are good baked, or stewed with meat. They may be served with boiled ham, salt cod, or any boiled meat.

CARROTS

These may be cooked as parsnips, to accompany boiled beef or mutton. Small ones will cook in an hour.

CABBAGE

All vegetables of this species should be carefully examined and washed, cut in two, and placed in cold water awhile, with a little common salt thrown into it. It is said that this will draw out the worms or insects and that they will sink to the bottom, so that greens or cabbages may be made free from anything of the kind. They should be boiled an hour or more, and the water pressed out before sent to the table. They should be kept in the cellar, or in a hole in the ground.

CAULIFLOWERS

Separate the green part, and cut the stalk close; let it soak a while in cold water, tie it in a cloth, and lay it in boiling milk and water, observing to skim it well. When tender, which will be in an hour and a half or two hours, take it up and drain it well; send it to the table with melted butter in a boat. Broccoli is cooked in the same manner.

RUTA BAGA

This turnip is large, of a redish color, and will boil in about two hours. Pare it, cut in quarters or slices, and let it be awhile in cold water. When boiled tender, cook them like other turnips; either mash them or send them to the table with melted butter over them in slices. It is said that the sun shining upon turnips, after they are cooked, will injure their taste.

BEETS

Wash them clean with a cloth, rubbing them well. Be careful not to cut them unless they are very large. If they are large, you may cut them in two, not splitting them. They require, when grown full size, three or four hours' boiling. When tender all through, scrape off the outside, split or cut them in thin round slices, and pour over melted butter and sprinkle with pepper. Boiled beets sliced, and put in spiced vinegar until pickled, are good. The tops of beets are good in summer boiled as greens. Beets should be kept in the cellar, covered with earth to keep them fresh. It is said that they are nicer roasted as potatoes for the table.

ONIONS

It is well to boil onions in milk and water, to diminish their strong taste. They require an hour or more, and when done, press out the water a little and season them with salt, pepper, and a little melted butter. They should be served hot, with baked or roasted meats. They should be kept in a dry place,

ANTI-MAGNETIC PROPERTIES OF THE ONION

The magnetic power of a compass needle will be entirely discharged or changed by being touched with the juice of an onion.

TOMATOES

If very ripe they may be skinned easily, but it is better done by pouring over them boiling water. Cut them fine, and lay them in a stew-pan with salt, a third of a teaspoon of pepper, and a piece of butter; cover them, and let them cook rapidly fifteen minutes. Have bread crumbs ready rubbed fine, and add to it while boiling; let it remain until they are soft, which will be, unless too hard, in two or three minutes; they must cook gently after the bread is in. They are good cooked in this way without the bread, but in that case they should stew uncovered and for longer. Prepared in the former manner is generally preferred, as it is less juicy. If cooled without the bread, they may be laid on a nice buttered toast, or sent to the table plain, They are kept best hung up on the vines in a dry place in the fall, as long as possible, but they should not be kept until they begin to decay. In Asia Minor they are preserved for use during the winter, in the following manner: Cut them in two, and sprinkle on them considerable fine salt to remain over night. Next day pass through a cullender. Set the part strained through to dry in the sun, in shallow dishes, in depth an inch or less. Dry it to more consistence than jelly, and put in covered jars for use. If it is not sufficiently dry to keep, add more salt and expose it again to the sun. A table-spoon will season a soup or stewed meats.

TO KEEP TOMATOES A YEAR

Take half a bushel, skin and boil them well, then add a teacup of salt, a tablespoon of black pepper, one tablespoon of Cayenne, an ounce of cloves, and an ounce of mace. Mix well, put them in jars, run mutton suit over them, and tie them up with strong paper or buckskin, and they will keep well, free from mold and acidity.

ASPARAGUS

Cut when two or three inches long, wash and place the heads all one way, and tie in bundles with thread or twine. Have your water boiling with a little salt and lay it in, keeping it boiling half or three quarters of an hour according to its age. Toast two slices of bread, moisten it with the water in which the asparagus is boiling, season with salt, and lay on a small platter or dish. Then drain the asparagus a moment, and, laying the heads inward, spread it on the toast, pouring over it melted butter and pepper.

GREEN PEAS

They are best when first gathered and shelled. They lose their flavor and sweetness by being kept; but if kept, do not shell them until they are needed. Put them in while the water boils, and only have just enough to cook them done. Season with salt, pepper, and a good supply of butter. If they have been kept, or if they are not a sweet kind, they are greatly improved by the addition of a spoonful of sugar, and, if a little old and yellow, a piece of saleratus. Another method is said to be an improvement: Place in your saucepan or boiler several leaves of head lettuce, put in your peas, with an ounce of butter to two quarts of peas; cover the pan or boiler close, and place it over the fire; in thirty minutes they are ready for the table. Season with pepper and salt, etc. It is said they are better than when cooked in water. Green peas should be boiled from twenty to sixty minutes according to their age.

STRING BEANS

Select only those that are tender, cut off the ends, and wash them well; take a handful and lay them even, and cut them very fine with a sharp knife upon a board or table. Put them in when the water boils, and if very tender they will require but half an hour; if not, longer. Season as peas.

SWEET CORN

This is sweeter for being boiled on the cob. If made into succotash, cut it from the cobs, and boil it with new shelled beans. It will require half an hour or more. Season with sweet cream or butter, salt, pepper, a little nutmeg, and a tablespoon of loaf sugar. It makes a most delightful dish to accompany a nice bit of boiled pork.

SPINACH

Pick it clean and wash in several waters. Drain and put it in boiling water, and be careful to remove the scum. When tender, drain and press it well. Chop it fine, and put in a sauce-pan with a piece of butter and a little pepper and salt. Set it on hot coals, and let it stew five minutes, stirring it all the time. It requires about ten minutes to boil.

EGG PLANT

The purple egg plant is better than the white. Boil them whole in plenty of water until tender, then take them up, drain them after having taken off the skins, cut them up, and wash them in a deep dish or pan; mix with them some grated bread, powdered sweet marjoram, a large piece of butter, and a few pounded cloves. Grate a layer of bread over the top and brown it in an oven. Send it to table in the same dish. It is generally eaten at breakfast. If you fry them, slice them, without being pared, about half an inch thick, and let them be an hour or two in salt water to remove their strong taste. Take them out, wipe them, and season with pepper and salt. Beat some yolk of egg and grate some bread crumbs. Have ready, in a frying pan, some lard and butter hot. Then dip the plant first in the eggs, then in the crumbs, till both sides are covered, and fry brown, taking care to have them done through, as otherwise they are very unpalatable.

VEGETABLE OYSTER OR SALSIFY

This excellent plant grows like a parsnip and is, in flavor, very much like fresh oysters. Scrape them, cut them round in thin slips, boil them tender in milk and water, and season them well with pepper, butter, and salt; make a nice toast, moistened with the gravy laid in the bottom of the dish, and pour the whole over it. You could scarcely detect the difference. There should be but a suitable quantity of the gravy; too much lessens the flavor. It is sometimes cut up and parboiled, chopped fine, and fried in batter. The roots may be first cooked tender, then fried whole in batter.

LIMA BEANS

Wash them and boil two hours or until they are soft; season with salt, pepper, and butter, not having much gravy. Use only water sufficient to boil them. They may be kept through the winter by gathering them on a dry day, before they are the least hard, and packing them in their pods in a keg. Throw salt in the bottom, then a layer of pods, then salt, then pods, until it is full. Press down with a heavy weight, cover the keg closely, and keep in a cool dry place. When used, soak them in the pods over night in cold water, the next day shell them, and soak until ready to boil.

DRY BEANS

Look them over, wash, and soak over night. Cut a new piece of salt fat pork, not too large, as it will make the beans too salty and hard; cut the rind in thin strips, change the water on the beans, and boil them together until the beans become soft. Take them out into a bean dish or deep dish of some kind, lay the pork in the center, having the rind just above the beans, pepper them, and have gravy enough to almost cover. It should be about even with the beans. Then set in an oven and bake an hour or until the pork is crisped. Some add a little molasses, and they are more healthy cooked with a little saleratus. Soft water should be used, if possible, to boil in, or saleratus is necessary.

DRY GREEN CORN

It must be gathered when just good to boil; strip off the husks and throw them in boiling water, and let them remain until the water boils over them. Then take them out and shell off the corn by running the prong of a long fork along the base of the grain. This method saves the kernel whole and is much more expeditious. Spread it thin on cloths in an airy, shaded place to dry, and stir it every day until thoroughly dry. When cooked, put it in cold water, and boil three hours. Let the water boil nearly off, add a little milk and sweet cream or butter, pepper, and salt, and it is very nice. If you wish succotash, soak dry white beans overnight and boil with them. It is a nice rare dish in winter and spring.

ARTICHOKES

Found to be very good when cut in thin slices with vinegar, salt, and pepper. If cooked, they must be boiled two or three hours closely covered and, when tender, served with melted butter.

FRIED CUCUMBERS

When pared, cut them in slices as thick as a dollar. Dry them with a cloth, season with pepper and salt, and sprinkle them well with flour. Have butter hot and lay them in. Fry of a light brown, and send to the table hot. They make a breakfast dish. When used raw, slice them into cold water to extract the unhealthy properties. Then season well with salt, pepper, and vinegar.

SEA KALE

This is prepared boiled, and served up as asparagus.

MUSHROOMS

Those of the right kind appear in August and September, after a heavy dew or misty night. They may be known by their pale pink or salmon color on the under side on the gills, while the top is a dull peach-colored white. They grow only in open places where the air is clear. After they have been gathered a few hours the pink color turns to brown. There should be the utmost care in selecting only those that are good, as the others are a deadly poison. They are of various colors, sometimes all white, or scarlet, or yellow. It is easy to detect them when fresh, but not after they have lain awhile.

DANDELIONS

When gathered young, they are good for greens. They require half an hour. Milkweed tops are very nice when cut young; these are both improved by cultivation. They require nearly an hour. Poke-root is good when it is first starting from the ground and is frequently brought to market. If at all too old it should not be eaten, as it is unwholesome. Boil it like asparagus one hour in plenty of water. Serve with or without toast, but with melted butter in a boat. Young horseradish leaves, dock leaves, plantain, patience, etc. make nice greens in the spring. They require about half an hour. Drain and press them, to accompany boiled meats.

EFFECTS OF VEGETABLES UPON ANIMALS

Horses that avoid the bland turnip will grow fat on rhubarb. Pigs will feed on henbane, but are destroyed by common pepper. Goats will feed on water-hemlock—though to other animals they are rank poison.

TOMATOES FOR COWS

This has been tried and is said will improve the quantity and richness of the milk, giving to the cream and butter a rich golden color, and will be found a cheap article of food.

MANAGEMENT OF PRODUCE

RADISHES

Wash them and let them lie in clean cold water as soon as they are brought in. Before they go to table scrape off the outside skin, trim the sharp end, leaveing the stalk about an inch long; if large, split them in four, half way down, and send them to the table in tumblers, to be eaten with salt.

CELERY

Scrape and wash it well, let it lie in cold water until just before used, dry it with a cloth, trim it, and split down the stalks almost to the bottom. Send it to table in a celery glass, and eat with salt only; or chop it fine and make a salad dressing for it.

LETTUCE

Strip off the outside leaves, split it and lay in cold water awhile. Drain and lay in a salad dish. Have ready two hard boiled eggs, cut in two, and lay on the leaves. If you choose, it may be dressed with sugar and vinegar, with a little salt, before it goes to the table. Some prefer a dressing of salt, mustard, loaf sugar, vinegar, sweet oil, and a mashed hard-boiled egg, with the salad cut fine and this over it.

COLDSLAW

Select the hardest, firmest head of cabbage. Cut it in two, and shave it as fine as possible. A cabbage cutter is the best. It must be done evenly and nicely. Lay it in a nice deep dish. Melt together vinegar, a small piece of butter, pepper, and a little salt. Let it scald and pour over it.

HOTSLAW

This is made in the same manner, except it is laid in a saucepan with the dressing, and just scalded but not boiled. Send it to table hot.

PICKLES

Kettles of block tin, or lined with porcelain, are best for pickling. Iron discolors the vinegar, and brass or copper, unless used with great care, is poisonous from the verdigris produced by acids. Pickles should always be covered with vinegar. If they show symptoms of not keeping well, scald the vinegar with fresh spices. Vinegar for pickles should never boil over five minutes, as it destroys the strength.

CUCUMBERS

Let your cucumbers be small, freshly gathered, and sound. Make a brine strong enough to bear up an egg, boil and skim it, pour upon the cucumbers, and let it stand twenty-four hours. Take good vinegar, cloves, cinnamon, and pepper, and boil together. Have your cucumbers in a large stone jar, and pour the hot spiced vinegar over them. If you wish them green, add a little alum with the spices to boil in the vinegar. Cover them well.

MELONS

To make mangoes of melons, you must gather them green and pour over them a boiling hot brine strong enough to bear an egg, and let them stand five or six days. Then slit them down on one side, take out all the seeds, and scrape them clean; then take cloves, ginger, nutmeg, or cinnamon and pepper, with small cucumbers and mustard seed, to fill them; sew them up with coarse thread, or tie them and lay them in a jar, and pour over them hot spiced vinegar. Cover them, and they will keep sound almost any length of time.

TOMATOES

They should not be very ripe. Mix in a stone jar an ounce of mustard, half an ounce of cloves, half an ounce of pepper, with half a jar of vinegar. Lay in the tomatoes with a dozen of onions and cover it close for a month. They will then be fit for use. If the jar is kept well covered, they will keep a year. The onions may be omitted if you choose and more spice substituted.

PEPPER

The bell pepper is considered best by some for pickling, and should be gathered when half grown. Slit one side and carefully take out the seed and core, so as not to injure the shell. Pour over them a strong hot brine, and keep them warm; some simmer them a whole day.

You may take them out next morning, when cool, and stuff them like mangoes, or lay them in a jar, with mustard sprinkled over them, and fill up the jar with vinegar. They require no spice, and should be pickled alone. The vinegar may be put on cold, with a piece of alum to give them a fine green, and it tends to harden and preserve pickles of any kind.

BUTTERNUTS

Gather them when they are easily penetrated by a pin, as early as July, when the sun is hot upon them; lay them in a tub with sufficient lye to cover them, and stir them round with a stiff broom to get off the roughness, or they may be scalded and rubbed with a cloth. Soak them in salt and water a week, then rinse and drain them. Pierce them through with a long needle, and lay them in a stone jar. Boil cloves, cinnamon, pepper, and ginger in the vinegar, and pour over them. Sprinkle through them two spoonsful of mustard seed previously, if you have it. They should be closely covered from the air. Walnuts may be pickled in the same way.

PEACHES

Take any kind of fine large peaches that are not too ripe, wipe off the down with a clean flannel, and lay them whole in a stone jar. Dissolve a tablespoon of salt to each quart of vinegar cold and cover them. Secure them well from the air. Plums, grapes, and barberries may be pickled in the same manner, without the salt, with the stems on. Add spices if you choose. They look beautiful, and barberries are sometimes used to garnish the edge of dishes.

CHERRIES

Use the common or Morelia cherries, pick off the stems, see that they are perfect, and lay them in a glass or earthen jar, with

sufficient cold vinegar to cover them; keep them in a cool place. They need no spices, as they retain their own flavor.

CAULIFLOWER

Select the whitest and closest full grown; cut off the stalk, divide the flower into eight or ten pieces, and scald them in strong salt and water; let them remain in the brine till next day. Then rinse and dry them. Lay them carefully in a jar not to break or crush them, and pour over them hot spiced vinegar. When the vinegar is cold, a few barberries or green grapes, put in the same jar, do not injure them, and add much to their beauty on the table. Broccoli and asparagus can be pickled much the same.

CABBAGE

Take red or white cabbage, quarter it lengthwise and crosswise. Select the firmest for pickling, and after it has lain in salt and water four days, drain it and pour over it hot vinegar, in which has been boiled cloves, mace, alspice, and pepper; if you wish to preserve the color of the red cabbage, put a little cochineal to brighten it, with a little alum. It will be more tender to repeat the scalding vinegar several times. Cover it closely.

ONIONS

Peel and soak them in salt and water three days. Then just scald them in milk and water, drain them, and dry them. Scald the spices with the vinegar, adding a piece of alum, and when cold pour over them. If kept in bottles, put a few spoonsful of sweet oil on the top. Cover close.

MARTINOES

The salt and water, in which they should be soaked two or three days, must be changed every day or they will become soft. Use alspice, cloves, and cinnamon, and scald the martinoes with the spices in the vinegar. Secure them from air.

NASTURTIONS

They should be gathered when full grown, but not old, and when the stems are taken off, wash them, and pickle in plain cold vinegar. Capers are done in the same manner. Both of these are best with boiled mutton.

RADISH PODS

Gather them in sprigs or bunches, young and tender, and after letting them stand in salt and water three days, pickle them like cucumbers.

GREEN BEANS

Gather them half grown and pickle in cold vinegar, with spices.

SAUERKRAUT

Cut cabbage fine, as if for slaw, then pack down in a cask; first lay down a sprinkling of salt, then a layer of the cabbage, then salt, then cabbage, until it is full, or nearly so. Then press it down closely, pounding it with something heavy to pack it close. Lay over it a round cover with a heavy to stone to ripen. It is not used until it has undergone a fermentation. When prepared for the table, it is fried in butter or nice dripping, and is with many a favorite dish.

HIGDOM

They are made of green melons, cucumbers, and onions. Take off the rinds and slice and chop them fine; green peppers are also used. Then add mustard-seed and spices. Press it into a jar, and cover with vinegar. In a week or two it will be ready for use. If onions are not agreeable leave them out. It is a nice pickle.

PARSLEY

May be tied in small bunches and pickled like cucumbers.

CHOPPED CABBAGE

When the heads are not close, chop them fine and season with red pepper, salt, and vinegar; it makes a very convenient and wholesome salad for the table.

EAST INDIA PICKLE

This is a combination of various pickles in the same jar. Take radish pods, green peppers, long and round, green grapes, capers, nasturtions, walnuts, butternuts, peaches, apricots, cherries, and button onions; pour over them a hot brine that will bear an egg, and let them stand four days, stirring them every day. Then make a pickle very warm with spices, and after it has been boiled and the ingredients well dried from the brine, pour it over them boiling hot; mustard-seed may be added, and then it must be covered close from the air. This will keep, if well prepared, two years.

Stone and wood are the only suitable materials in which to keep pickles. All pickles should be stirred up occasionally. When any scum rises, the vinegar needs scalding. When the vinegar becomes weak it should be thrown away, with new substituted in its place. Good, though not sharp, vinegar is best for pickling. If brass or copper is used in preparing pickles, it should.be thoroughly cleansed before using with vinegar and salt, and no vinegar allowed to cool in them, as it would then be poisonous.

Cucumbers may be preserved in salt or brine for any length of time. But there should be a weight upon them to keep them well covered, or they will become soft. When prepared for pickling they must be soaked and scalded. No salt will be needed in the vinegar.

TO PICKLE OYSTERS

Take those that are large, separate them from their liquor, and pour over them boiling water; take them out and rinse them. Put them in a kettle with just water enough to cover them, a tablespoon of salt to every hundred oysters, and just let them boil up. Take them out on a large board and cover them with a cloth. Take the liquor of the oysters, and with every pint mix a quart of the best vinegar, a tablespoon of whole cloves, the same of whole black pepper, a teaspoon of whole mace. Heat the liquor, and when it boils, put in the oysters and stir them five minutes. Then let them cool. When cold, put them in jars and cover them securely.

TO PICKLE MUSHROOMS

Wipe them carefully, put them in an earthen vessel, and sprinkle salt over them; let them stand for eight hours. Put them in a pan and strain the liquor to them; let them boil till nearly dry. Take them out and lay between clean cloths. Boil some

good vinegar with pepper and mace, put the mushrooms in, and give them a boil up; put them into glass bottles, and cork tight.

ASSUMPTIONS WITH CATCHUPS

TOMATOE CATCHUP

Take six pounds of tomatoes and sprinkle with salt; let them remain a day or two, then boil, and press through a coarse sieve or cullender. Put into the liquor half a pint of vinegar, cloves, pepper, ginger, and cinnamon, and boil them one third away; bottle tight. It should be shook before being used.

MUSHROOM CATCHUP

Take the full grown tops of mushrooms, wash clean, crush them, throw a handful of salt with every peck, and let them stand all night. Put them in a stew pan and let them stand in a quick oven twelve hours. Strain them through a hair sieve to press out all the juice. To every gallon of liquor put an ounce each of cloves, Jamaica or black pepper, and ginger and half a pound of salt. Set it on a slow fire to boil until half gone; then, when cooled in an earthen vessel, bottle for use. It sometimes needs boiling the second time to keep long.

WALNUT CATCHUP

Take a peck of green walnut shells, put them in a tub, bruise and mash them, and throw on two or three pounds of salt; add enough water enough to cover them. Let them stand six days, straining and mixing them until they become soft and pulpy. Drain out the juice by letting the tub stand on one side a little, with the shells in the elevated part. As often as it needs, turn out the liquor and continue it as long as there is any, which will be five or six quarts. Then boil it in iron as long as scum arises; then add a quarter of a pound of ginger and allspice and two ounces of pepper and cloves, and let it boil slowly half an hour. The spices should be powdered, and a quantity of it should go into each bottle. Cork them tightly and put them in a cool dry place one year before it is used.

PUDDING CATCHUP

Mix together half a pint of noyau, a pint of wine, the yellow peel of four lemons pared thin, and half an ounce of mace. Put the whole in a large bottle, and let it stand two or three weeks. Then strain and add a strong syrup of sugar. Bottle it, and it will keep two or three years. It may be used for pudding sauce, mixed with melted butter, and various other sweet dishes.

THE MANY MAKINGS OF VINEGAR

WHISKEY VINEGAR

Take five gallons of soft clean water, two quarts of whiskey, two quarts of molasses, and half a pint of good fresh yeast. Lay a sheet of white paper at the bottom of the keg and put in the mixture. Place it in the warm sun, and in six weeks it will be fit for use. If made in winter, it should be kept where there is a fire.

CIDER VINEGAR

This may be made of poor cider, or that which is good, weakened a little with water. It should be partly drawn off, after the cider is well worked, leaving the casks about two-thirds full. A piece of wire gauze, or a linen cloth let in a little, should be nailed over for a cover to keep out flies, and also for a strainer. When the vinegar is good, which will be sometime in six months by frequent shaking, it may be increased by adding occasionally the juice of fruit, the rinsings of sweetmeat jars, cold tea, etc.

SUGAR VINEGAR

To each gallon of water, add two pounds of brown sugar and a little yeast; expose it to the sun six months in a vessel slightly stopped.

HONEY VINEGAR.

Mix one pound of honey with a gallon of cider and expose it to the sun, or keep it where it is warm, and in a few months it will be so strong that water will be necessary to dilute it.

PERRY VINEGAR

Put thirty or forty pounds of wild pears in a tub, pour water over them, and leave them three days to ferment. Repeat this every day for a month, at the end of which it will be good vinegar.

RASPBERRY VINEGAR

Mix a quart of the best vinegar with two quarts of fine red raspberries; let it stand for nine days, or longer if not fermented; then strain them through a fine sieve, and to every pint of liquor add three quarters of a pound of fine sugar; simmer it gently and finish by boiling quickly for twenty minutes. This makes a pleasant drink with cold water.

Chapter 6: IN REGARDS TO BEVERAGES

HOW TO MAKE BEER

WHITE SPRUCE BEER

Three pounds of loaf sugar, five gallons of water, with enough essence of spruce to give it a flavor, a cup of good yeast, and a little lemon-peel if you choose; when fermented, bottle it up close. It is a delightful beverage in warm weather.

GINGER BEER

One cup of ginger, one pint of molasses, one pail and a half of water, and a cup of lively yeast. In warm weather it may be made cold, but, in cold weather, scald the ginger with two quarts of hot water, and the rest cold. The yeast should be put in when slightly warm. It should be put in jars or bottles and securely corked. It is pleasant and lively and will keep several weeks.

COMMON SMALL BEER

A handful of hops to a pailful of water, a pint of bran, half a pint of molasses, a cup of yeast, and a spoonful of ginger.

ROOT BEER

Take a pint of bran, a handful of
hops, some twigs of spruce, hemlock, or
cedar, a little sassafras, or not as you
have it, roots of various kinds, plantains,
burdocks, dock, dandelions, etc.; boil
and strain and add a spoonful of ginger
molasses, to make it pleasant, and a cup
of yeast. When you want it soon, let one
bottle stand where it is warm, and the rest will work cold. This for a
gallon.

MOLASSES BEER

Six quarts of water; two quarts of molasses; half a pint of yeast;
two spoonsful of cream tartar. Stir all together. Add the grated peel of
a lemon; and the juice may be substituted for the cream tartar. Bottle
after standing ten or twelve hours, with a raisin in each.

TO RESTORE ACID BEER

Stir in a small quantity of saleratus with a spoonful of sugar, and it
is even richer and better than at first. To be prepared as you use it.

HOW TO MAKE COFFEE

PARISIAN COFFEE

This is made by leeching. Many prefer it to any other mode. It is
very easily made and requires nothing to settle it. Any common coffee
pot will answer the purpose, with a strainer formed to fit the top. It
is made in form like a cup with fine a strainer made by piercing the
bottom full of small holes very fine, and above that another not as
fine, on which the ground coffee is laid. Pour on boiling water, using

the same quantity as in other modes, and cover it close, when the water is all drained through, which will be in ten minutes or less, it is ready for the table. Some have biggins made in the French mode, but the other answers the same purpose and is equally good. It should stand near the fire while cooking. It will leave the dregs tasteless.

THE COMMON METHOD

A general rule. Allow one tablespoon of ground coffee per person. Have your coffee pot free of old dregs and well rinsed. Old grounds spoil the taste. Wet your ground coffee with cold water, and add a piece of fish skin as big as a shilling or a piece of a porkrind. Or you can stir in a part of an egg, not more than a spoonful, as more prevents the strength of the coffee from extracting. It forms a mass when a whole egg is used and cooks around the coffee, so that about half the strength is lost. Pour on boiling water and let it boil ten or fifteen minutes, pour out a cup full and pour it back to clear the spout if you do not use an urn. Take it from the coals, and let it settle a few moments, before sending it to the table. Have rich sweet cream or boiled milk, with the yolk of an egg stirred into it (if you'd like), and

good sugar. This mode of preparation will be equally good as French coffee.

Great care is necessary in roasting it; unevenly or overly roasted will spoil it; and if it is not sufficiently brown, it will be insipid and wanting in flavor. There is also a great difference in the kinds of coffee. Some is better flavored than others. The green and small is generally best.

To have coffee very good, it should be browned just before it is made, though this is an inconvenience. Pick out the stones and bad grains, and lay in a dripping pan or tin, allowing layer to dry. Set it in an oven after baking, or under a stove a few hours, and then put it in a spider on hot coals and stir it constantly until the color of rosewood or black walnut. Stir in a small piece of butter, put up, and cover it immediately, as it evaporates fast while hot. Never grind until just before using.

OTHER SUITABLE POTATIONS

MOLASSES, ETC

Take new sweet cider just from the press, made from sweet apples, and boil it down as thick as West India molasses. Four or five barrels will make one of good molasses. It should be boiled in brass and not burned, as that would injure the flavor. It will keep in the cellar, and is said to be as good and for many purposes better than West India molasses.

HARVEST DRINK

Mix with five gallons of good water, half a gallon of molasses, one quart of vinegar, and two ounces of powdered ginger. This will make not only a very pleasant beverage, but one highly invigorating and healthful.

LEMONADE

Take good lemons and roll them; then cut and squeeze them into a pitcher. Add loaf sugar and cold water till it makes a pleasant drink. It should be sweet; it is sometimes too acidic to be agreeable. Send round in small glasses with handles or tumblers a little more than half full. The best drink for parties.

ORANGEADE

This is made in the same manner as lemonade.

TO PRESERVE LEMON PEEL

A pint of lemon juice to a pound of powdered loaf sugar. When all melted, bottle close and keep in a dry place.

ESSENCE OF LEMON PEEL

Grate off the rinds of lemons with loaf sugar in lumps until the yellow part is all off. Take it up as fast as you proceed, and put it in a cup or china jar, and cover it closely. Oranges may be prepared in the same way. It may be used for cakes, pies, puddings, etc.

CHOCOLATE

To a quart of water, allow three spoonsful of scraped chocolate. Let it boil fifteen or twenty minutes and stir while boiling. Pour in rich cream or milk and let it boil up. Some like nutmeg grated over a cup, and I think it improves the flavor.

COCOA

This is similar to chocolate but is more delicate. It is much used by those who cannot drink coffee and tea.

The directions for making come with the article on the wrapper.

TEA

If green tea is good, it will look green when poured into the cups. Black tea should have a fragrant flowery smell. Allow one teaspoon to a person, and one beside. Have the water boiling, scald the teapot, and put in the tea as soon as possible; cover it and let it draw about five minutes; old Hyson requires longer. Black tea should boil ten minutes. Have sweet cream and loaf sugar, or the best common, crushed. There should be but a small quantity of water used to draw the tea, and it should be filled up afterwards. Black tea is healthier than green. Mixed with the other kinds, half and half, is a good practice.

TO PRESERVE MILK

Put a spoonful of horseradish into a pan of milk, and it will remain sweet for several days, either in the open air or in a cellar, while other milk will sour.

MILKING

One steady hand that will do it quick and easy should always milk. It should be done at regular hours, and care should be taken to do it clean.

SIMPLE MODE OF PURIFYING WATER

A tablespoon of powdered alum, sprinkled into hogshead of water and stirred, will in the course of a few hours precipitate to the bottom all the impure particles and leave the water as clean and pure as spring water. Four gallons would need but a teaspoonful.

TO MAKE WATER COLD DURING SUMMER

It may be kept nearly as cold as ice water by surrounding the pitcher or jar with several folds of coarse cotton, to be constantly wet. The evaporation carries off the heat inside, and it will be reduced almost to freezing. In India and other tropical regions this is common.

TO MAKE HONEY WATER

Put two drachms of tincture of ambergris and as much tincture of musk into a quart of rectified spirits of wine, and half a pint of water. Put it in small bottles for use.

CHAPTER 7: WHEN BAKING BREAD, BREAKFAST, TEA CAKES, ETC

YEAST

Boil a single handful of hops and a sliced potato in three pints of water. In fifteen or twenty minutes strain it out boiling hot on two pints of flour, stirring it well. When it is so cool that it will not scald, put in a teacup of light yeast and a little ginger; when the whole is raised, put in sifted meal, as much as can be kneaded. Then take it upon your board, work it into rolls, and cut it in thin slices; lay them on tins to dry. Be careful not to scald them while drying. When done, put it in a bag and you will have the best of yeast. Soak it at night and stir in a little flour. In the morning it will be ready for use. This is preferable to any other, at any season of the year. It cannot be affected by heat or cold, if kept in a liquid state, the same yeast may be put in a close jar or jug and will make excellent bread.

MILK YEAST

Take half a pint of boiling water and half a pint of sweet milk; stir in flour to make a batter nearly as thick as fritters. Set in a kettle of warm water, keeping it at the same temperature, and in about four or five hours it will rise and be fit for use. It must be used immediately. Make your bread with warm milk or water, put it in your pans, and it will rise in an hour. Made in the same way without milk, with the addition of a teaspoon of salt and a teaspoon of sugar, will make bread equally good. They are both nice in warm weather. They make bread or biscuit very white, and some prefer it to any other.

TO MAKE BROWN BREAD

Two quarts of lukewarm water, a half teacup of molasses, a cup of yeast; wet it up stiff; when light, add a teaspoon of saleratus. This is for two loaves.

INDIAN GRIDDLES

One quart of milk, one pint of Indian meal, four eggs, four spoons of flour, and a little salt; beat it well together and bake on a griddle or pan. Another way is to take equal parts of flour and Indian meal and a little salt; wet it in a thick batter with some milk or buttermilk and a teaspoon of saleatus—bake as above.

BANNOCK

Two cups of meal, two of flour, a teaspoon of salt, one of ginger, four spoonsful of molasses; wet with buttermilk, a teaspoon of saleratus. Bake an hour.

"SPLENDID JOHNNY CAKE"

Take one quart of milk, three eggs, one teaspoon of saleratus, one teacup of flour, and enough Indian meal to make a batter as thick as pancakes. Bake quick in pans, well buttered. Eat warm, with butter or milk. Those who may not have eggs will find they are very good without. The milk should be sour or buttermilk.

POTATO YEAST

To a pound of mashed potatoes add two ounces of brown sugar and two spoonsful of common yeast. The potatoes must be pulped through a cullender and mixed with warm water to a proper consistence. This will make a quart of good yeast. It must be kept moderately warm while fermenting. If yeast is kept in a liquid state, it should be corked close in a jug, when suitably light, or in a close jar. A little salt and ginger added to the yeast, when you put it away, will improve it.

TO KEEP HOPS

Hops lose their fine flavor by exposure to the air and damp. They should be kept in a dry close place and lightly packed.

TO MAKE DELECTABLE BREAD WITH GROWN FLOUR

Take eight quarts of flour, six ounces of butter, one pint of yeast of the best kind, and three teaspoons of saleratus dissolved in half a pint of warm milk; add this to the yeast, and, after working the butter into the flour, add the yeast and just enough milk to make the bread stiff. Knead the whole together. Bread made of grown flour must always be made harder or stiffer than any other kind. In this way good bread may be made. It should rise and bake like other bread.

PLAIN FRITTERS

Take a quart of buttermilk, or sour milk, a pint or more of sweet milk, three beaten eggs, a teaspoon of salt, and a teaspoon of saleratus; stir in flour enough to make a thick batter. Have your lard hot, drop them neatly by the spoonful into the lard, and fry them a light brown. Serve them with liquid pudding sauce, sprinkle sugar and nutmeg over them, or serve plain.

TEA BISCUIT

Take two cups of cream, one of sour milk, a teaspoon of salt, and one heaping teaspoon of saleratus dissolved, stirred in last. Mix as soft as possible to roll, cut with a tumbler, and bake in a quick oven half an hour. This will fill one tin. If you have no cream, use half sour milk, and half melted butter, or clean dripping instead, which will be equivalent to cream, though not quite so nice.

EXCELLENT APPLE FRITTERS

Pare your apples, cut in thin slices, and mix them with your flour. Stir in a quart of milk and four eggs, a little salt, and saleratus, to make a thick batter. Fry in plenty of lard.

CREAM FRITTERS

Take a quart of sweet milk and a teacup of cream, four eggs beat to a froth, half a nutmeg or grated lemon peel, and a teaspoon of salt. Stir them with flour sufficient to make a thick batter, dissolve a small teaspoon of saleratus, and stir in, then fry as above.

BUCKWHEAT CAKES

Mix a quart of flour with a pint of lukewarm milk (some prefer water), add a teacup of yeast, and set in a warm place to rise. In the morning, if sour, add a teaspoon of saleratus and a little salt. Bake as griddles and butter when hot. These are nice for breakfast or with butter and sugar for tea. When you make them every day, leave a little in the jar, and it will raise the next.

SODA BISCUIT

To one quart of flour add two teaspoons of cream of tartar, dissolve a teaspoon of soda in sufficient water to wet the flour. They may be made in a few moments and are very nice with coffee for breakfast.

OYSTER-CORN CAKES

Take one quart of green corn, rasped from the ear with a coarse grater, two teacups of milk, one teacup of flour, and two eggs well beaten. Season the batter with salt and pepper and bake on a griddle. This makes a capital dish.

MOCK OYSTERS

This is similar. Grate twelve ears of corn, wash the cobs in a teacup of milk; add to this three eggs, two spoonsful of flour, one teaspoon of salt, and bake as above. They have the flavor of oysters and are very nice.

HOT ROLLS

Dry your flour before the fire, add a little warm milk, with two spoonsful of yeast, an egg well beaten, and a little salt. Let it stand all night and bake the rolls in a quick oven.

HOE CAKE

Scald a quart of Indian meal, with just water enough to make a thick batter. Stir in two teaspoons of butter. Bake in a buttered pan half an hour.

RICE CAKES

Boil a cup of rice to a jelly, add a little milk, two spoonsful of butter, a little salt, four eggs well beaten, and flour to make a batter. Fry as other griddles, and serve hot, with powdered sugar and nutmeg. Another way is to take rice, boiled in the usual way, and make them like flour pancakes, only use a little flour. They are white and nice.

WAFFLES

Beat four eggs; mix flour and milk enough to make a thick batter, using a quart of flour, a tablespoon of melted butter, and a teaspoon of salt. Bake in waffle irons and season with melted butter and sugar, flavored with nutmeg, lemon, or cinnamon. They may be made with a part of boiled rice or like common griddles.

GRIDDLE CAKES

Take a pint of thick milk, or a quart of sour; to the thick add a pint of sweet milk, a little salt, a teaspoon of saleratus, and flour to make a batter. The thinner the batter, if baked well, the more tender they will be. Half a teacup of cream improves them. Butter while hot and serve with sugar, honey, or maple molasses. For a common sauce, take a teacup of cream, a spoonful of sugar, and half a teaspoon of ginger. It is a delightful way of eating them.

CRUMPETS

Take three teacups of raised dough and work into it half a teacup of melted butter, three eggs, and milk to make a thick batter. Bake in a hot buttered pan in half an hour.

WAFER CAKES

These are nice for tea. Take two-thirds of a teacup of butter, the same of sugar, three well beaten eggs, and a teaspoon of rose water. Make a stiff batter, and, when well beat and smooth, have your wafer-irons hot and well buttered, then fill them and close tight; place in the fire to cook both sides at once, and they will be done in ten minutes.

A RETIRED BAKER'S RECEIPT FOR BREAD

Take an earthen vessel, larger at the top than at the bottom, put in one pint of warm, water one and a half pounds of flour, and half a pint of malt yeast; mix well together, and set away in a warm place until it rises and falls again, which will be in three to five hours. Then put two large spoonsful of salt into two quarts of water, and mix with the above; when it's rising, put in about nine pounds of flour and work it well; let it rise until light, then make it into loaves. New and runny flour requires one-fourth more salt than old and dry flour. Bake as soon as light.

GRAHAM OR DYSPEPSIA BREAD

Take three quarts of unbolted wheat flour, one quart of warm water, one gill of fresh yeast, one gill of molasses, and one teaspoon of saleratus. Make two loaves, bake one hour, and cool gradually. No bread should be put in an oven too hot, as it will prevent its rising as it ought.

COMMON DOMESTIC BREAD

Take three quarts of warm milk or water, a teaspoon of salt, a teacup of light, foamy yeast; stir in enough flour to make a thick batter, and let it stand and rise until light. Then, if a little sour, add a tea-spoon of dissolved saleratus; if very sour, add three. Grease four tins and do up the bread in loaves, after kneading it well, and let it rise again on the tins. When just light enough, bake in an oven or stove well heated, but not too hot. It will be done in three quarters of an hour. For biscuit, work into dough enough for a loaf and a cup of butter and do up small. If dripping is used, two-thirds of a cup is enough.

BROWN BREAD

Take Indian meal sifted and wheat or rye flour, equal parts, a cup of yeast, and two spoonsful of molasses. Some scald the meal and

others wet it with warm milk or water. Add a little salt and place it in pans to rise. It should be wet soft, if the meal is not scalded, stirred with a spoon; but harder otherwise.

TOAST WITHOUT BUTTER

Prepare bread in the usual way; put in a pan a pint of new milk, and when the milk in the pan boils, have two tablespoons of flour dissolved smooth in a little cold milk and pour in; add a teaspoon of salt, let it scald, but not boil, and pour it over the bread.

MILK TOAST

Boil a pint of rich milk with a tablespoon of butter and one of flour. Have ready in a dish eight or ten slices of bread toasted. Pour the milk over them hot, and cover it until it goes to the table.

JOHNNY CAKES

Take a quart of sour milk, thick or otherwise, a teaspoon of salt, sifted meal to make a stiff batter, a teaspoon heaping full of dissolved saleratus, with or without a spoonful of flour. Butter a pan, and bake nearly an hour. For tea, it is improved by adding half a teacup of molasses, a little allspice, and a spoonful of cream or shortening.

A WARM LOAF FOR BREAKFAST

Make as above: put in an iron basin with an iron cover and place in the kitchen fireplace; when the fire is raked for the night, put fire and hot ashes around and over it, and in the morning you will have a nice, warm, brown loaf.

MUFFINS

One pound of flour, one pint of milk, a teacup of butter, the same of yeast, and two eggs. Bake without tins.

MUFFINS ANOTHER WAY

Take a quart of warm milk, half a cup of melted butter, four eggs well beaten, a teaspoon of salt, a spoonful of yeast, and flour to make a batter. Let it stand covered in a warm place two hours. Grease your rings, fill them half full, and bake moderately.

VARIOUS KINDS OF PLEASANT CAKES

FRUIT CAKE

Take one pint of light dough; one teacup of sugar; one of butter; three eggs; a teaspoonful of saleratus; one pound of raisins; nutmeg or cinnamon, to the taste; bake one hour. Let it stand and rise a little before baked.

FRENCH LOAF

Three teacups of light bread; two cups of white sugar; one cup of butter; three eggs; one nutmeg; one small teaspoon of saleratus. Rub the butter and sugar together, add the egg, and lastly add the bread and fruit. Bake in a loaf one hour and a half.

SPONGE CAKE

Ten eggs; their weight in sugar; the weight of seven eggs in flour. Beat the whites and yolks separately, then add sugar and flour. Before baking, add the juice of one lemon and one teaspoon of saleratus.

COURT CAKE

Four eggs; two cups of sugar; one of butter; one of buttermilk; half a teaspoon of saleratus; half a nutmeg; put them together and beat them well. Add one pound of fruit and three cups of flour. When sufficiently beaten, add the saleratus and bake nearly an hour.

CUPCAKE

One cup of sugar; one of butter; three and a half of flour; four eggs and a half a cup of cream; half a teaspoon of saleratus. Bake in a loaf or small tins.

MEASURE CAKE

Two eggs; one cup of sugar; half a cup of butter; half a cup of cream; two cups and a half of flour; half a nutmeg; and half a teaspoon of saleratus. Let it be well beat and add the saleratus last. Bake nearly an hour.

CONVENTION CAKE

One teacup of butter; two cups of sugar; three of flour; four eggs; beat well. Try it, and all kinds of cake, with a fiber from a corn broom inserted through the middle of the loaf. If nothing adheres it is done, and if there does, let it remain until done.

POUND CAKE

One pound of flour; one pound of sugar; one pound of butter; eight eggs; three spoonsful of rose water or without; beat it well and bake three quarters of an hour.

COOKIES

One cup of cream; half a cup of butter; one and a half of sugar; one teaspoon of pearlash; two eggs; wet as soft as you can roll, and bake quick. Caraway seed if you please.

RICH PLUM CAKE

Mix two quarts of flour with a pound of sifted loaf sugar; three pounds of currants; half a pound of raisins, stoned and chopped; a quarter of an ounce of mace and cloves; a grated nutmeg; the peel of a lemon cut fine; melt two pounds of butter in a pint and a quarter of cream, but not hot; the whites and yolks of twelve eggs beaten apart; and half a pint of good yeast. Beat them together a full hour. Put in a plenty of citron and lemon. Then butter your hoop or pans and bake.

SHREWSBURY CAKE

One pound of flour; three quarters of a pound of sugar; three of butter; four eggs; beat till very light; bake moderately.

SOFT CAKE IN LITTLE PANS

One cup and a half of sugar; the same of butter; eight eggs; and half a nutmeg; or without if preferred.

A LIGHT CAKE TO BAKE IN CUPS

Half a pound of sugar; half a pound of butter, rubbed in two pounds of flour; one glass of wine or rose water; two of yeast; one of nutmeg; and fruit if you please.

QUEEN'S CAKE

Whip a cup and a half of butter to a cream; add two cups of sugar; eight eggs; flour, to make suitably stiff; beat well and bake in a good oven not over half an hour. It may be dropped on tins, with currants laid in the tops.

SUPPLEMENTARY QUEEN'S CAKE

One pound of flour; one of sugar; three fourths of butter; five eggs; a gill of cream; mace and nutmeg baked in small tins with or without currants or sultana raisins. Ice them and flavor the icing with lemon or rose.

SCOTCH CAKE

Stir to a cream two cups of sugar and a cup and a half of butter; put in the juice and grated rind of a lemon. Beat nine eggs to a froth and stir in; add enough sifted flour to make it a stiff batter. If you wish it very nice, add a quarter of a pound of citron cut in thin pieces and almonds blanched and powdered fine in rose water. Bake in pans, or drop on tins two inches apart, with white sugar grated over them.

A SIMPLE SPONGE CAKE

Take twelve eggs; two cups of powdered loaf sugar; the grated rind of a fresh lemon, and half its juice; beat to a stiff froth; then add two cups of sifted flour, and bake in a quick oven, but not too hot. It will bake in twenty minutes.

JUMBLES

Take six eggs; a cup and a half of sugar; one of butter; beat it to a froth; add lemon or rose water, and flour enough to roll; cut out with a large tumbler, and cut out the middle with the top of a small canister, to leave a perfect ring. They should be rolled in white powdered sugar and baked on tins in a quick oven.

KISSES

Beat the whites of four eggs to a stiff froth; add the juice of a lemon or a little rose water. Roll and sift half a pound of the whitest loaf sugar and beat it with the egg. Spread out white paper on tins buttered, and drop a tablespoon of this mixture on the paper. The oven should be only moderately hot, and when the tops have become hard, remove them. Have a solution of gum Arabic, dip the lower side of the cake, and join it to another.

HONEY CAKE

Three quarters of a pound of honey; half a pound of fine loaf sugar; a quarter of citron; a half ounce of orange peel cut small; of cinnamon and ginger, each half an ounce; four well beat eggs; and a pound of sifted flour. Melt the sugar with the honey and mix. Roll out the cakes, and cut in any form.

ALMOND BRIDE CAKE

Take four pounds of flour, sifted, four pounds of butter, two pounds of loaf sugar, sifted fine, a quarter of an ounce of nutmegs, and the same of mace; to every pound of flour put eight eggs; wash and pick four pounds of currants and dry them; blanch a pound of sweet almonds, and cut them lengthwise, very thin; ready a pound of citron, a pound of candied orange, and a pound of candied lemon. Beat the butter with the hand to a cream, then add the sugar, and beat a quarter of an hour; beat your eggs to a strong froth and stir in; then add the flour, mace, and nutmeg, and heat till the oven is ready; at last stir the almonds and currants lightly in and bake in well buttered pans or hoops. It will take, if the loaves are large, three hours baking.

COCOANUT CAKES

Take equal parts of grated cocoanut and powdered white sugar; add the whites of eggs, beaten to a stiff froth, half a dozen to a pound. There should be just eggs enough to wet the whole stiff. Drop the mixture on buttered tins, in parcels of the size of a cent, several inches apart. Bake them immediately in a moderate oven.

A CHOICE WEDDING CAKE

One pound of flour, one of sugar, one of butter, twelve eggs, two pounds of raisins, two pounds of currants, a pound of citron, lemon, nutmeg, and mace, to your taste. Beat it all very light. Flour the fruit and stir in last and, if necessary, add more flour. Have one large pan or two smaller ones well buttered, put in a layer of the cake, and then one of citron sliced thin, and so on until full. It will need a well heated and steady oven to bake four or five hours according to its thickness. Let it cool gradually in the oven. Ice it when thoroughly cold.

POTATOE CHEESE-CAKES

Half a pound of potatoes, boiled and rubbed through a sieve, half a pound of butter, beaten to a cream, half a pound of white sugar, the yolks of six eggs, and twenty drops of the essence of lemon. The eggs should be beaten separate and added the last thing. Line a dish with good paste and pour the mixture in. Bake half an hour.

LEMON CHEESE-CAKES

A quarter of a pound of butter, three quarters of a pound of sugar, six eggs, the grated rind of two lemons, and juice of three. Put all these into a pan, over a slow fire, gently stirring it, till as thick as a good cream; then pour it into jars and tie them down close. Keep it in a dry place, and it will be good for a year. Line a dish with paste, as above.

SPONGE GINGERBREAD

A pint of molasses, a teacup of sour milk or buttermilk, a tablespoon of ginger, two spoonsful of melted butter, two teaspoons of saleratus dissolved, and flour sufficient to roll. Cut it about half an inch thick, and bake in a quick oven.

SOFT GINGERBREAD

One cup of cream, one of molasses, a teaspoon of ginger, one of saleratus dissolved, a little salt. Bake in half an hour.

GINGERNUTS

One cup of molasses, half a cup of sugar, a spoonful of ginger, one cup of butter, half a cup of sour milk, two teaspoons of saleratus dissolved in boiling water and stirred in after the flour. Make it just stiff enough to roll very thin; cut in small cakes and bake in a slow oven.

BAKERS' GINGERBREAD

Four ounces of saleratus dissolved, and put in a gallon of good molasses and four spoonsful of ginger mixed with sufficient flour; have four ounces of alum pounded and dissolved in a small quantity of boiling water, kept boiling until wanted, and pour in last. Rub in the flour and two pounds of butter. Make it as soft as can be rolled, and cut in cards.

PLUM CAKE

One pound of butter beat to a cream; one pound of sugar; twelve eggs, leave out two whites. Beat separately and then mix together. Add one pound of flour; one glass of brandy or wine; two pounds of currants; two of raisins; one and a half of citron. Flour the first and when ready to bake, put in one ounce of

mace; two of cloves; half an ounce of cinnamon and nutmeg. Just as you bake it, add a teaspoon of saleratus dissolved and a tablespoon of molasses.

A GENUINE SPONGE CAKE

Seven eggs; twelve ounces of sugar; six of flour; a little rose water; if you please, a spoonful of wine.

COOKIES

Six cups of flour; three of sugar; one of butter; one of sour cream; one of sour milk; a teaspoon of saleratus and one of caraway seed.

FRUIT GINGERBREAD

Four cups of flour; one of butter; one of sugar; one of molasses; one of milk; four eggs; three teaspoons of ginger; a teaspoon of cloves and nutmeg; half a pound of currants and raisins. Add the fruit last, and bake in pans in an oven not very quick.

WASHINGTON CAKE

Beat six eggs very light; add one pound of butter; a pound of sugar; a pint of rich milk or cream a little sour; a glass of wine; powdered nutmeg; a spoonful of cinnamon; and lastly, a small teaspoon of saleratus. Bake in tins or small pans in a brisk oven, and if wrapped in a thick cloth, it will keep soft a week.

JELLY CAKE

Make a pound cake with a little less flour than usual. Beat it well and have rather a thin batter. Lay your griddle in the oven of a stove, and place on it a cake ring well buttered, as large as a dinner plate, or use small muffin rings; have the griddle well buttered and lay in two large spoonsful and a half of the cake batter; bake about five minutes and turn; proceed thus until it is all baked, and when cool spread them with jelly, or marmalade, and put two together; fill a plate and cut in triangular pieces. It is best when fresh.

INDIAN POUNDCAKE

Take a pint of sifted meal; a half pint of flour; nutmeg and cinnamon. Beat eight eggs; a half pound of sugar; the same of butter; and stir in gradually. Beat well together and bake an hour and a half. It should be eaten fresh and is then very nice.

WHITE CUP CAKE

Take four cups of flour; two of white sugar; one of butter; one of sour cream or rich milk; nutmeg, cinnamon, and lemon, with five well beaten eggs; and lastly a small teaspoon of saleratus. Bake in cups or tins in a moderate oven twenty minutes.

CRULLERS

Six eggs; one cup of butter; one and a half of sugar, cinnamon, nutmeg, and rose water. Beat well, and stir in flour enough to roll into any fanciful shape. Fry a light brown in a plenty of lard. When cold, grate over them loaf sugar. Another way to make them is to take one egg; four spoonsful of sugar; three of butter; one cup of cream; salt and spices to your taste. Fry in lard.

AN EXCELLENT COMMON FRIED CAKE

One cup of sugar; one of cream; three eggs; cinnamon or nutmeg; a teaspoon of saleratus. Cut as jumbles, or in strips, twisted, and fried in lard.

EXCELLENT PLAIN CRULLERS

One cup of shortening; one of molasses or sugar; one of sour milk; one egg, if convenient; a teaspoon of cinnamon, ginger, or nutmeg; a little salt; a teaspoon of saleratus, dissolved in half a cup of hot water. Fried as above.

DOUGHNUTS

One cup of butter; one of sugar; nutmeg, cinnamon, or rose water and two eggs; worked into a quart bowlful of bread dough, on light sponge; make as hard as biscuit and let it rise an hour or more; add a teaspoon of saleratus to the sponge. When light, cut in squares or balls, and fry six or eight minutes in hot lard. They should be a mahogany brown. The New York "Oley Koeks" are doughnuts with currants and raisins in them.

AN EXTENSIVE LOOK AT CAKES

CAKES

One pound of fresh butter, one pound of sugar, two pounds of flour, two pounds of currants, three quarters of a pound of candied citron, lemon and orange, a quarter of a pound of sweet almonds blanched and chopped, ten eggs, and one ounce of mixed spice. Melt the butter to a cream, add the sugar and spice, and beat for a quarter of an hour. Add the yolks of the eggs, two or three at a time; the whites should be beaten to a strong froth, and worked in gradually; then add the fruit and almonds and flour. Bake three hours.

QUEEN-CAKE

Fourteen eggs, one pound of fresh butter, one pound of flour, one pound of sugar; the yolks and whites should be beaten separately. Add half a pound of currants or candied peel.

RICE-CAKE

Half a pound of butter, half a pound of sugar, six eggs, a quarter of a pound of flour, a quarter of a pound of rice flour. Melt the butter to a cream, add your sugar, stir it till it is light, break in six eggs, two at a time, and keep stirring your paste all the time; when the eggs are worked, add the ground rice and flour. Bake this in a hoop, in the same way as a plum-cake.

THICK GINGERBREAD

Half a pound of flour, a quarter of a pound of butter two ounces of sugar, one pound of molasses, half an ounce of ground ginger, a quarter of an ounce of saleratus dissolved in a teaspoon of warm milk. Rub butter, sugar, and ginger well in the flour; add the molasses and saleratus the last thing.

GINGERBREAD CAKES

A pound and a half
of flour, half a pound of
moist sugar, half a pound
of butter, two ounces
of ginger—rubbed well
together, and mixed with
three quarters of a pound
of molasses.

HONEYCOMB GINGERBREAD

Half a pound of flour, half a pound of moist sugar, a quarter of a pound of butter, half an ounce of ginger, half the peel of one lemon grated, and all the juice. Mix all together to a paste with half a pound of molasses; make it thin enough to spread upon sheet tins rubbed with butter; bake it in a moderately hot oven, and watch it all the time. When baked, it must be cut upon the tins, with a knife, in strips, and rolled around a wafer-stick. It will keep good for a month in a very dry place and closely covered.

POUND-CAKE

One pound of flour, one pound of butter, one pound of sugar, one pound of eggs, half a pound of citron. Beat the butter to a cream, then add the sugar and yolks of eggs, a few at a time, then the whites. Beat all well together, stir the flour lightly in, and the citron the last thing.

ALMOND-CAKES

One pound of fine flour, three quarters of a pound of loaf sugar sifted, two eggs, half a pound of butter, a quarter of a pound of currants, one ounce of bitter almonds blanched and pounded. Mix all well together and make into small cakes. Bake about ten minutes.

SHREWSBURY CAKES

Half a pound of butter, half a pound of flour, three quarters of a pound of sifted sugar, one egg, a quarter of an ounce of carraway seeds. Mix all these ingredients well together, make into a paste and roll out thin, using as little flour as possible; cut them out with a round cutter and bake in a hot oven.

RUSKS

Half a pound of sugar, seven eggs, six ounces of flour, one ounce of carraway seeds (carraway seeds are optional). The eggs should be very fresh. Beat the whites to a strong froth, whisk in the yolks and powdered sugar and seeds. The flour should be stirred gently in with a spoon. Bake in buttered moulds, in a warm oven. When cold, cut them in slices, and brown them in a hot oven, first on one side, then on the other.

MACAROONS

One pound of sweet almonds, a pound and a quarter of sugar sifted, six whites of eggs, and the rasping of two lemons. Pound the almonds very fine with the whites of eggs; when quite smooth, add the sugar and lemon raspings; have some wafer-paper on flat baking-sheets, and place the paste in small lumps on it. Bake them in a moderately-heated oven. When cold, cut the paper round them. They should be kept in a dry place.

SPONGE-CAKE

Twelve eggs, twelve ounces of flour, one pound of sugar, and the raspings of two lemons. Beat the yolks, lemon, and sugar well together for twenty minutes, beat the whites to a strong froth, and pour the batter into it, then add the flour very lightly.

A VERY NICE CAKE

Six. eggs, half the whites, two ounces of sugar sifted, a quarter of a pound of flour, a quarter of an ounce of sweet almonds, and half an ounce of bitter almonds pounded fine. The sugar, yolks of eggs, and almonds to be well mixed, the whites beaten separately, and the flour added the last thing. To be baked in a quick oven, half an hour.

TEA-CAKES

Two pounds of flour, a quarter of a pound of butter rubbed in the flour, one pint of milk, one egg, a teaspoon of sugar, and a little yeast—made into a light dough and set to rise. This is sufficient for twelve large cakes.

PIES, PUDDINGS, ETC.

MINCED PIE

Boil fresh beef perfectly tender, that will slip off the bone. The head and harslet are nice for this purpose. Take out all the hard gristle and bone and tough parts when hot. As soon as it is cold, chop it all very fine, and if you do not want it for immediate use, season it with pepper, salt, cloves, and cinnamon, press it closely into a stone jar, and pour molasses over the top. When after a few days or weeks it has left the surface, pour on more to keep it nice. To every two quarts of chopped meat, a half a teacup of ground cinnamon, a tablespoon of ground cloves, a teaspoon of pepper, and a tablespoon of salt will keep it well, with molasses poured over it, a year. It is far more convenient to have meat thus prepared for use through the winter than to boil every time it is needed. The proportions should be a third meat and two thirds apple, chopped very fine, those a little sour are best. A good mince pie is a general favorite, and formerly brandy was deemed indispensable in giving them the right flavor. But we are happy to inform our temperance friends and others that a mince pie can be made equally good without either wine or brandy. Add a good quantity of box raisins and season high with spices and molasses, adding water sufficient to keep them moist, made up in a rich nice paste, and there will be nothing wanting in flavor or quality. They should be baked one hour in a moderate oven.

MINCE MEAT

Four pounds of raisins, four pounds of currants, four pounds of apples chopped fine, four pounds of beef suet, three pounds of beef, four ounces of citron, four ounces of orange and lemon candied, two nutmegs, two ounces of cloves and allspice, half an ounce of cinnamon, one pound of white sugar. Mix all well together.

DRIED APPLE PIE

Stew the apples soft, turn them into a pan, and mash them fine. Add half the peel of a lemon cut fine, or a little grated nutmeg, a sprinkle of salt, molasses, or sugar to make them quite sweet. Bake them in a rich paste a little over half an hour. This will be quite as good as fresh fruit.

GREEN APPLE PIE

Stew and strain the apples, grate the peel of a fresh lemon, or rose water and sugar, to your taste. Bake in a rich paste half an hour.

A BUTTERED APPLE PIE

Pare and slice tart apples, lay them in a rich paste, and bake half an hour. When done, raise the top crust and add sugar, a little butter, and flavor with lemon, rose water, nutmeg, or cinnamon. They are best when fresh baked.

CURRANT PIE

Take green currants, pick, and wash, add one third their quantity in sugar and raisins. Add half a teacup of water to each pie, and a single handful of flour sprinkled over the fruit. They are sometimes made without any other fruit. Dried apples stewed are a good substitute for raisins, and if used alone, molasses is better than sugar. Pies made of berries are better without spices.

CHERRY PIE

Stone your cherries, that you may be sure they are free from worms. Lay your paste in a deep dish, and add a good quantity of fruit; fill the dish with molasses, with a handful of flour sprinkled over, then a nice paste, and bake more than half an hour. If sugar is used, you will need water and flour. This makes the gravy very rich and the pie delightful.

RHUBARB PIE

Take the tender stalks of the rhubarb, strip off the skin, and cut the stalk into small pieces. Line your plate with a rich paste, and put in a layer of rhubarb and a thick layer of sugar, and so on until filled; a little lemon peel improves the flavor. Cover with a crust cut in the middle, or prick it that the juice of the pie may not run out. They must be baked an hour in a slow oven. Some stew it beforehand, and in that case they will bake in half an hour. But if they are wanting in sugar, they will not be good; see that there is no deficiency in this respect, and they are very nice.

PUMPKIN PIE

Pare and stew the pumpkin soft, let it remain over the fire, stirring it often until quite dry. When cool strain through a sieve or fine cullender, and add milk about one quart to one of pumpkin. Let it warm after they are strained together, then add molasses or sugar, a little salt, nutmeg, cinnamon, or lemon, with a spoonful of ginger and an egg or two with a handful of flour. Bake in a hot oven nearly an hour.

POTATO PIE

Boil common or sweet potatoes until well done. Mash and strain them; to a pint of the potatoes, add a pint and half of milk, half a teacup of sweet cream, or a little melted butter, two eggs, and sugar, salt, nutmeg, or lemon, to the taste.

APPLE CUSTARD PIE

Grate four sweet apples for every large pie, a pint and half of milk, two eggs, sugar, a little salt, nutmeg or lemon, to the taste. Bake as a custard pie in a quick oven.

LEMON PIE

Take one lemon, slice very thin, lay it in a rich paste. Sprinkle over it one spoonful of four and one teacup of sugar; fill the pie nearly full of water and cover. Bake in a slow oven nearly an hour.

RED SUGAR BEET PIE

Pies made of the red sugar beet are said to be delicious, somewhat resembling rhubarb pie in flavor, though more rich and substantial. It is seasoned with vinegar, sugar, and spices to suit the palate. The root may be used without boiling, being chopped fine. Prepare the crust, and bake as you would a green apple pie.

COCONUT PIE

Grate the white part and mix with milk. Let it boil slowly eight or ten minutes. To a pint and half of cocoanut, add a quart of milk, four eggs, half a cup of sweet cream, two spoonsful of melted butter, a cracker rolled fine, and half a nutmeg. The cocoanut should cool before the eggs and sugar are stewed in. Bake in a deep plate like a custard in a quick oven.

BUTTERNUT PIE

Twelve butternuts dried and pounded, made like custard pie, in other respects, is rich and nice.

A PLAIN CUSTARD PIE

The crust of all custard pies, or those made like custard, should be made with the addition of a little sour milk and saleratus to make it light, and then it will never be soaked and wet at the bottom. It is a great improvement. To every two pies, allow five eggs, sugar nutmeg, lemon, salt, to the taste, and bake in a quick oven.

TOMATO PIES

Take ripe tomatoes, skin, and slice. Sprinkle over a little salt, and let them stand a few minutes; pour off the juice and add sugar, half a cup of cream, one egg, nutmeg, and cover with a rich paste. Bake in a moderate oven over half an hour. This makes an excellent and much approved pie.

TARTS

Cut out the paste with a tumbler, then cut strips of paste to lay round the top neatly, press it in the middle to form it deeper, then lay in sweetmeats, etc. and bake on tins.

ORANGE OR LEMON TART

Cut in slices and boil six large lemons or oranges with a little salt two or three hours until perfectly tender. Then take six pippins, or other good apples, pare, quarter and core, and boil them until they begin to break; then put them together with a pound of sugar, and boil together a quarter of an hour. Lay this in a puff paste, rich and nice, sift over them superfine sugar, and bake, and they will be delightful.

EGG PUDDING

One quart of milk, nine eggs, nine spoonful of flour, a little salt; put in a bag and boil in boiling water one hour and a half. Use a liquid sauce or one made of butter sugar and nutmeg mashed together.

FLOUR PUDDING

One quart of milk scalded. Dissolve a pint and half of flour with cold milk and two spoonful of sweet cream and when free from lumps, stir it into the scalded milk. Beat seven eggs, a little salt, sugar to your taste, half a nutmeg or cinnamon. It may be either baked or boiled. It takes two hours to boil, and an hour and a quarter to bake. If boiled the bag should be only two thirds full, That it may swell. It must be put in boiling water and kept boiling. It must be turned in ten minutes or it will be heavy. If baked, and raisins are used, they should not be put in until the pudding has cooked enough to thicken, or they will settle at the bottom. Flour pudding should be eaten as soon as cooked, or they will fall. Serve with a nutmeg sauce made as above.

CREAM ALMOND PUDDING

One quart of sweet cream. Beat eight eggs, and mix with them eight spoonsful of flour and one quarter of a pound of almond; when settled, add one spoonful rose water, half a nutmeg, a little cinnamon, and beat well together. Wet the bag, or flour the inside, and boil an hour and a half. Serve with melted butter and sugar.

POTATOE PUDDING

One pint and a half of boiled mashed potatoes, a teacup of sugar, half a teacup of butter or sweet cream, one cup of flour, one quart of milk, and four eggs. Flavor with lemon peel, nutmeg or rosewater, a little salt, and bake one hour or more.

PLUM PUDDING BOILED

Three pints of flour, six eggs, one pound of plums, a teacup of chopped beef suet, a teacup of sugar, one pint of milk. Mix the whole together. Flour the bag, and boil three hours. Serve with a rich sauce.

A PLAIN RICE PUDDING

Boil a pint of rice; add a quart of new milk, halt a cup of butter, four spoonsful of sugar; boil them up together and let them partially cool. Beat five eggs well and stir in, and, if raisins are added, let them be stirred round after it has partly cooked, so that they do not settle at the bottom. Flavor with salt, cinnamon, or nutmeg, and bake one hour.

PUFF PUDDING

Take six eggs, six spoonsful of flour, one quart of milk, and half a teaspoon of saleratus . Bake twenty minutes. Serve with sauce as soon as baked. It is very light. Some bake in cups and turn out in a dish.

A BOILED RICE PUDDING

Boil a pint and a half of rice with half a pound of raisins; when the rice is soft, if there is water remaining, pour it off, and add a quart of rich milk. Let it boil five minutes, and then add four spoonsful of sugar and two eggs well beat, stirring it until the rice and eggs are well mixed. Season with a little salt, nutmeg, or cinnamon, and it makes an excellent and easy dish. It should boil five minutes and be stirred often.

SOUTHERN MODE OF BOILING RICE

Have the water boiling. Allow at least a quart of water to a pint of rice; throw in a teaspoon of salt; wash and pick clean and put in; let it boil twenty minutes, and if not then dry, turn off the water, and let it stand on the coals a few moments with the lid off. The kernels will be white and preferred by many. Use in the place of pudding, with a sweet sauce, or with meats as a vegetable.

A RICE PUDDING, GOOD WITHOUT EGGS

A teacup of dry rice to a quart of milk. Season with a little salt, sugar, nutmeg, and if you please raisins, and bake two hours. It will be very nice.

ENGLISH PLUM PUDDING

Soak a pint of crackers in a quart of milk; the crackers should be rolled. When they have become soft, add half a teacup of melted butter, four spoonsful of sugar, a gill of wheat flour, half a wine glass of wine, and half a grated nutmeg. Beat five eggs to a froth, and stir them into milk. Add a quarter of a pound of seeded raisins, the same of Zante currants, and two ounces of citron cut in strips. Bake or boil two hours.

ORANGE PUDDING

Grate two large oranges and squeeze their juice. Beat six fresh eggs, and stir them into a teacup of melted butter and the same of white powdered sugar. After that, add the orange, with half a pint of cream, and lay in a rich puff paste in a deep plate or pudding dish, and bake like custard. Lemons may be used in the same way.

QUINCE PUDDING

Pare, core, and chop four large quinces; boil until perfectly soft, then mix with a pint of cream, a teacup of sugar, six eggs well beat, a glass of rose water, and a little salt. Lay it in a buttered dish, and bake an hour or more.

SAGO PUDDING

Soak six tablespoons two hours in cold water, then boil it in a quart of milk till quite soft. Stir in half a teacup of butter, and one of white sugar, and let it cool. Beat eight eggs very light, and stir them into the sago, etc. Season with lemon, rose water, or nutmeg, and add currants well floured or raisins. Stir the whole, and lay in a buttered dish, and bake in three quarters of an hour. It may be served cold.

"BIRD'S NEST" PUDDING

Take eight or ten pleasant apples and dig out the cores, leaving them whole. Prepare a custard, six eggs to a quart, flavor with lemon, orange, or nutmeg and a little salt, and when the apples are laid in a pudding dish, pour the custard over them, and bake half an hour

BAKED BREAD PUDDING

Cut slices (or broken pieces of bread are equally good) and soak in milk until soft. Then add two eggs to a quart, a little salt or butter, lemon peel, nutmeg, or

cinnamon, and sugar. Bake an hour. This is wholesome, and best for common use.

BAKED INDIAN PUDDING

Scald the milk, and stir in the sifted meal to make a batter not very thick. Then add two spoonsful of flour, molasses to your taste, a little salt, lemon, nutmeg, or cinnamon, and bake two hours and a half. Made in this way, it is quite as good as when made with eggs.

TO BOIL RICE WHOLE

Have a quart of water boiling hot, with half a teaspoon of salt. Wash a pint of rice and throw in; let it boil twenty minutes. If the water is not evaporated, pour it off, and let it stand on coals two minutes. It is then ready for the table. Serve with a sauce flavored with nutmeg.

A BOILED APPLE PUDDING

Boil dried apples nearly done. Save a teacup of the juice of the apple for a sauce. Chop them, and mix with soaked bread, and boil in a bag. Make a sauce of melted butter, sugar, and flour, with enough of the apple juice to give it the flavor of wine, and spice with nutmeg. It is excellent.

PLUM PUDDING

One pound of flour, half a pound of suet chopped fine, half a pound of raisins, half a pound of currants, a quarter of a pound of sugar, two ounces of candied peel, the rind of a lemon grated, a pinch of salt, some nutmeg. Mix well together, and make into a stiff batter, with three eggs and a little milk. Boil three hours.

CARROT PUDDING

Half a pound of flour, six ounces of suet chopped, half a pound of currants, three tablespoons of sugar, a little spice of candied peel, half a pound of carrots, well boiled and rubbed through a sieve. Mix the other ingredients, thoroughly; then add the carrots; boil four hours.

LEMON PUDDING

The rind of one lemon, boiled tender and beat fine, with a little raw peel grated, six ounces of sugar sifted, four ounces of butter melted. Mix all together well, then add the yolks of six eggs, well beaten. Line a dish with paste, pour the mixture in, and bake half an hour.

TAPIOCA PUDDING

A pint and a half of new milk, a teacup of tapioca, and two ounces of sugar, to be put together, and boil five minutes; then pour it into a basin. When cold, add four whole eggs, well beaten; flavor with the essence of lemon, or what you please. Put the mixture into a well-buttered mold, and steam it for an hour. It is excellent when cold with preserved fruit.

CUP PUDDING

Half a pound of butter, half a pound of flour, half a pound of sugar, half a pound of eggs; mix the eggs and sugar, then add the flour, and afterward the butter, which must first be beaten to a cream; to be baked in cups, in a quick oven, twenty-five minutes.

MACARONI DRESSED FOR A PUDDING

Boil two ounces in a pint of milk, with a bit of lemon peel and a good bit

of cinnamon, till the pipes are swelled to their utmost size without breaking. Lay them into a custard dish and pour a custard over it. Serve cold.

HASTY PUDDING

Have your water boiling hot, put in a spoonful of salt, then stir in sifted meal until the stick will stand in it. Stir in the meal and let it boil awhile, then finish it, and let it boil slowly fifteen minutes. It is good with butter and molasses hot, or with milk. When cold it is nice for breakfast, cut off in slices and browned in a frying pan, with a little butter or fresh sweet lard or dripping.

HOMINY

Wash it until the chaff is well out, which will rise on the surface of the water. Put it in cold water, and boil it four or five hours over a slow fire. Add a spoonful of salt. It is very good with milk, sugar, or molasses. It is much esteemed by children, and good for delicate persons.

MACARONI

Put a piece of butter, half a pound of macaroni, and a little salt into hot water, and let it boil three quarters of an hour. Drain it and put it in another saucepan, with butter and grated cheese. Toss up the whole together, adding two or three spoonsful of cream, and when done, put it on a dish and send to table hot.

APPLE DUMPLINGS

Lay into rolled paste, apples quartered and cored; roll up and boil in a cloth one hour. Serve with a sauce made of melted butter and sugar, flavored with nutmeg. Another method: Lay the apples in a small kettle with water sufficient to boil them tender, with the paste over. Cover it close, and boil half an hour. Serve with sauce. One more: Lay the quarters in paste cut round, and tie up in cloths to make them like "snow balls." Serve with the same sauce.

BAKED APPLE DUMPLINGS

Take a pint of stewed apple sifted; those that are a little tart are best. Add two cups of sugar, eight eggs, half a cup of butter, one quart of milk, and rose water, lemon, nutmeg, or cinnamon to your taste. Bake one hour.

ICE CREAMS, CUSTARDS, ETC.

ICE CREAMS

Mix two tablespoons of arrowroot powder or fine starch, with milk sufficient to make a thin paste, stirring it till perfectly smooth. Boil together a pint of cream and a pint of milk, and, while boiling, stir in the preparation of arrowroot and let it boil aagain. Then take it off and stir in half a pound of loaf sugar, and let it boil again. If vanilla is preferred, take the half of a bean, split it in pieces, and boil it in a little milk to extract the flavor and stir in with the arrowroot but if lemon, add a few drops after it is boiled; if strawberry is preferred, express the juice of a quart of ripe strawberries, and add to the powdered sugar, to boil with the whole. Then strain and put in a freezer, placed in a tub that has a hole in the bottom to let out the water, and surround the freezer on all sides with broken ice and coarse salt. While freezing, stir it well half an hour, scraping it down

from the sides. When frozen, transfer it to a mould, surround it with fresh salt and ice, and freeze it over again. Another method is to take one pint of cream, three pints of new milk, one pound of loaf sugar, two lemons, and half of a vanilla bean. Boil and stir the sugar in gradually. If you have no lemon, use four eggs. Freeze as above.

SNOW CREAM

Beat the whites of four eggs to a froth; and stir in two spoonsful of white sugar; flavor with rose water or lemon; add a pint of thick sweet cream; and beat the whole together, to a froth. This is to be served with a desert of sweet meats.

WHIP CREAM

Take a pint and a half of cream; the whites of three eggs; white sugar to your taste; and a part of the juice of a lemon; then whip it with a whisk made of a bunch of quills or in a whip churn; flavored with the rind of grated lemon or rose water; and as the foam rises, lay it into jelly glases. If preferred, the glass may be half filled with jelly, and the whip poured over it.

LEMON CREAM

Take a pint of thick cream; the yolks of two eggs well beaten; a cup of white sugar; and the rind of a lemon cut thin; boil it up. Then stir it until almost cold. Put the juice of a lemon in a dish, and pour the cream upon it, stirring well until cold. Serve in a large glass dish, or in custard cups, either alone or with sweetmeats.

ORANGE CREAM

Pare and squeeze two oranges on a cup of finely powdered sugar with half a cup of water. Beat four eggs well, add, and beat them together some time. Strain the whole through flannel into a saucepan; set it over a gentle fire, and stir it one way until thick and scalding hot—not boiling or it will curdle. If lumps of sugar are rubbed hard on the lemons before they are pared, the flavor will be better extracted; or they may be grated. Serve as a custard in jelly glasses.

SNOW CUSTAD

Make a rich custard; eight eggs to a quart of new milk; a gill of sweet cream; a little salt; and flavored with lemon, nutmeg, orange, or rose water; boil until just thick, and lay in a dessert or pudding dish with a whip over the whole. Serve as you would a pudding.

GOOSEBERRY OR APPLE CUSTARD

Boil your fruit, pulp it through a sieve, season with sugar, and flavor the apple with grated lemon or nutmeg. Lay a thick layer of the fruit in a dish and mix a pint of milk, a pint of sweet cream, and then yolks of two eggs. Scald it over the fire, stirring it; add sugar to the taste and let it get cold. Lay it over the fruit with a spoon, and over the whole a whip. Some prefer the whip made the day before.

CHARLOTTE DE RUSSE

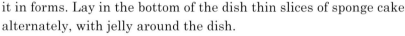

Take six eggs to a pint of milk; add sugar to sweeten it. Strain into it an ounce of dissolved isinglass; when baked let it cool, make a whip, and mix with the custard; cool it in forms. Lay in the bottom of the dish thin slices of sponge cake alternately, with jelly around the dish.

TRANSPARENT LEMON JELLY

Pare two dozen as thin as possible. Put eight lemons with the rinds into hot—not boiling—water, and cover it three or four hours. Rub some loaf sugar on the rinds before peeling, to extract the flavor. Put in a china dish with a pound and half of fine sugar, then add the water and three quarts of boiling milk; mix and pour through a jelly bag until clear.

JELLY FROM FEET

Boil four calves feet. When they have boiled to pieces, strain through the cullender; when cold, take off the grease. There, should be two quarts of the jelly; put this in the skillet, add one quart of white wine, one pound and a half of powdered white sugar, the rinds of two lemons. Wash the outside of eight eggs, crush shells and all, and put them in. Stir it occasionally until it is melted, but do not touch it after. When it has boiled to look quite clear, then get a pitcher under, and if you choose, place it afterward in molds. The bag should be made of cotton.

BLANC MANGE

Break one ounce of isinglass in very small pieces and wash well. Pour on a pint of boiling water; next morning add a quart of milk, and boil until the isinglass is dissolved and strain it. Put in two ounces of blanched almonds pounded, sweeten with loaf sugar and turn in the mold, stick thin slips of almonds all over the blanc mange, and dress around with syllabub or whip cream.

FLUMMERY

Four calves feet well cleansed, add four quarts of water and boil down to one. Strain it, and when cold, take off the top and the sediment. Then add a pint of cream, a little rose water or lemon, sweeten to your taste, boil up and pour into cups to stiffen.

ANOTHER LEMON JELLY

Pare four lemons, squeeze the juice and strain it, put the rinds and juice in a quart of water and sweeten with loaf sugar to your taste, add the white of six eggs beat to a froth. Set it over the fire and stir until it thickens, but not to boil. When cold strain through a sieve, put on the fire, add the yolk of the eggs, stir till thick, and serve up in glasses.

ANOTHER BLANC MANGE

Take one ounce of isinglass, two quarts of milk, the peel of two lemons, sugar and spice to suit the taste. When dissolved partly, bring the whole to a boiling heat, strain it, and when nearly cool, stir it well to raise the cream so that it will rise while cooling. Pour it into molds first wet with cold water. It is best to make it the day before it is used; if it does not slip out easily, wrap a cloth wet in hot water around the molds, then loosen it with a knife and turn out into glass dishes. It may be set to cool in teacups or wine glasses, and if you prefer it, may be stained: green, with the juice of spinach; yellow, with saffron; red, with cochineal, infused a half hour in a little brandy.

PLUM AND CHERRY CHARLOTTE

Stone a quart of ripe plums or cherries, and combine them with a pound of brown sugar. Cut slices of bread and butler, and lay them round the sides and in the bottom of a large deep dish. Pour in the fruit boiling hot, cover the bowl, and set it a way to cool gradually. When quite cold, serve with sweet cream. This is very nice in hot weather.

RASPBERRY CHARLOTTE

Take a dozen of oblong sponge cake, commonly called Naples biscuit. Spread over each a thick layer of raspberry jam, and place them round and in the bottom of a glass bowl. Take a pint of cream and eight spoonsful of raspberry, or currant jelly, and beat together, and fill up the bowl with it. If you have not cream, take the white of six eggs, and six spoonsful of jelly, and beat very light in the same way. A charlotte may be made with any kind of fruit jelly, marmalade, or jam. It can be prepared at short notice, as it is a favorite dish.

CONVENIENT TABLE JELLIES

Use three good sized lemons cut in thin slices, the skin off from one. Take one pound of white sugar, two quarts of cold water, two ounces of isinglass previously soaked half an hour, spices to suit the taste. If you wish it transparent add the white of three or four eggs. Stir it well, and boil the whole one minute, then pour through a jelly bag, ten inches across, narrowing to a point at the bottom. The liquid that runs first should be poured back until it runs clear. For wine jelly, add one pint; the liquid from preserves and fruit jellies, may be used according to taste. Put into glasses or molds previously wet; when cold it is ready for use.

TAPIOCA PUDDING

To one pint of water, add a teacup of tapioca, and soak over night. In the morning add two beaten eggs, three pints of milk, and bake as any other. Another: Half a pint of tapioca dissolved in a quart of milk while boiling. Add six eggs when nearly cold, with nutmeg or cinnamon. Bake ten or fifteen minutes.

GREEN CORN PUDDING

Grate or cut the corn from the cob fine. To the corn of two dozen ears, add half a pint of milk and a quarter of a pound of sugar; when mixed, bake an hour and a half, or until the crust is brown. Eat simply with butter; some add pepper.

APPLE CUSTARD

Pare, core, and slice twelve pippins. Boil a pint of water, a pound of loaf sugar, and twelve cloves, and skim. Put in the apples and stew until the liquid is nearly gone. Lay them in a deep dish, take out the cloves when they are cold, pour in a quart of custard, and let it cook by setting the dish in boiling water until it sets. The same with quince but more sugar.

NELSON'S PATENT "OPAQUE GELATINE"

Soak one ounce of opaque gelatine in half a pint of cold water ten minutes. Then add the same quantity of boiling water, stir it until dissolved, and add the juice and peel of two lemons, with wine and sugar to make one quart. Stir in the white and shell of an egg, well beat together. Then boil it five minutes without stirring it. Remove it from the fire two minutes and strain through a close flannel bag. This is highly recommended for blanc mange, and all kinds of jellies. It is said to be in every respect better and cheaper than isinglass or other gelatines. One ounce will form a quart of calves foot, mange, lemon, and other jellies sufficiently firm to turn out of molds. It is also used in soups with less meat.

FLOATING ISLAND

Take the white of an egg or more as you want; beat to a froth, add a glass of currant jelly, beat them together until a spoon will stand up in it. Drop a spoonful at a time on a glass bowl of sweet cream.

TO MAKE WAFERS

Mix flour and water to a thick paste, and have your flat irons at a moderate heat; lay on just oil enough to keep them from sticking. Place one between a couple of common chairs with the face upward, color the paste with Venetian, or vermilion, or prussian blue, and lay a very small quantity on the face of the iron, have the face of the other oiled and set it on the other, and it will press it out and scald it through. Take this off and continue the process until finished. Have something prepared to cut them with, and you have perfect wafers. If they are not cut they answer a good purpose for papers, etc. They will be thick or thin according to the quantity used of the paste. Half a teacup will make a large supply.

ARROWROOT BLANC MANGE

Take a teacup of arrowroot, dissolve in a little cold water. Take half a pint of new milk, sweeten with loaf sugar to your taste. If you want it very sweet, add the grated peel of a lemon, a grated nutmeg, and pounded mace, and boil until highly flavored. Strain into a pint of milk and half a pint of cream; add two thirds of a cup of sugar, and boil ten minutes; then strain it boiling hot into the arrowroot. After the water has been poured off, stir it constantly until thick, and then put in molds to congeal.

COLD CUSTARD

Soak a piece of rennet in wine, and you will be able to have custard at any time without eggs or cooking it. Sweeten and flavor a quart of sweet rich milk; if you like, add a little salt. Then stir in a spoonful or two of the rennet wine, and turn into cups. When it is thick like a rice custard, grate over a little nutmeg, and you will have a delicate custard.

LEMON CREAM

Take the rinds of two lemons, cut them, put them into a pint of cold water, let it stand all night, squeeze the juice into the water, sweeten to your taste, beat the whites of six eggs to a strong froth, put all together into a pan, stir over a very slow fire till warm—not hot enough to curdle—stir gently till cold, and put into glasses. It should be made several hours previous to being served.

LEMON ICE

For a quart mold, take a pint and half of water, the rind of three lemons, and three and a quarter pounds of loaf sugar; boil for ten minutes. When nearly cold, add the yolks of eight eggs and juice of eight lemons, well beaten together; mix like a custard—freeze it in the usual manner—it is excellent. Orange ice may be made in the same way.

CUSTARD ICE

Make a nice, smooth custard, with the yolks of ten eggs to a pint and half of thin cream. Flavor with what you please. When half frozen, add some dried fruit, cut in small pieces; mix up, and finish freezing.

RULES FOR PRESERVING

All delicate fruit should be done gently, and not allowed to remain more than half an hour before it is laid on a dish to cool and then returned. Continue so until transparent. Put no more in the pan than can lie without crowding. A pound of sugar to a pound of fruit, is a general rule for acidic fruit. Preserving kettles should be broad rather than deep. The flavor of the fruit is preserved by covering the kettle. If sweet meats become candied, set the jar in water, and let it boil around it. Tissue paper cut to nicely fit over the top, is better to preserve from mold, etc. than white paper wet with brandy. To clarify sugar: to every eight pounds of sugar, stir into two quarts of water the whites of two eggs, and mix with the sugar. While it is melting, stir frequently. Then place it over a moderate fire, and as it boils take off the scum. When clear, put in your fruit as above. Large fruit that is done whole should first be boiled in a thin syrup, or it will shrink too much. Small fruit is best to stew half the sugar over it, and let it stand a day or night.

QUINCES

Pare and cut in eight quarter pieces; boil until tender in a little water; turn them in an earthen vessel, and let them remain one day. Then boil and strain the parings and pits or seeds, which will afford a rich jelly liquid; to this, add your sugar, clarify, and when hot, lay in your fruit, and scald it an hour gently. Skim it out, and boil the liquid until sufficiently thick, and pour over. If you have cut few quinces, prepare one third or half the quantity of the same sized apples cut in the same manner, cook in the sugar syrup first, and lay in the bottom of the jar, and they cannot be told from the quince in flavor. If you wish to make quince jelly do not boil the cores with your preserves, but reserve them for this purpose, and add a few pieces of the quince, to give it a higher flavor. It will make a rich, clear, delightful jelly, with the usual amount of sugar made in the usual way. Some prefer quinces cut in rings.

PEACHES

If you preserve them whole, they should be gathered before they are fully ripe, and before they part from the stone. Pare them, and boil in the syrup gently, until they are tender. If in quarters, crack the pits of half the peaches and boil in the syrup; strain and cook in the usual way. Put up in jars and glasses. Some prefer them cooked in a little water, and the syrup poured over them hot. Jelly may be made in the usual way; mash them, and strain through a jelly bag. Allow a pint of juice to a pound of loaf sugar, and if it does not readily congeal, dissolve an ounce or more of isinglass, strain, and add. Put up in tumblers. The kernels should be cracked, and half of them boiled with the fruit.

If you wish them preserved in brandy, they should be gathered before they are ripe, rubbed with flannel, pricked with a large needle to the pit, in several places, and the need should have been run down the seam. Put them in cold water and boil them very gently until tender. Take them carefully out, fold them in a table cloth or soft flannel. Have ready a pint of brandy; a pint of the juice, in which they were boiled; a pound of loaf sugar. When the peaches are cool lay them in a jar and pour over them. They may be used as a dessert.

PEARS

These look best if moderate size, preserved whole, pared, with the stems on. Make a thin syrup, and boil them tender. If boiled too fast, they will break. They will be sufficiently cooked in half an hour. If you wish them nice, let them lie in the syrup in a jar or tureen two days. Drain the syrup from the pears; add more sugar; boil ten minutes; skim, and put in the pears; simmer them till they are transparent. Take them out; stick a clove in the end of each; and lay in a jar when cool. Then pour over the warm syrup. For common use, they are best done in quarters, boiled tender in a little water; then add half a pound of sugar to a pound of pears to the liquor, and simmer them gently half an hour. They may be flavored with lemon if preferred. They are nice for common use, baked. They may be done with the stems on and pared or with the skins. Put them in a tin with half a teacup of molasses and the same of water, or the same of sugar and water. They will bake in an hour.

PLUMS

May be preserved nice with the skins on or off. If on, they should be pricked at the top and bottom with a large needle. If you take them off, turn boiling water over them. Plums require a pound and a half of sugar to a pound of fruit. Prepare your syrup thick, and lay in your plums to simmer, not to boil; let them remain in a scalding state until cooked through, at least two hours. Then skim out and boil the liquor down about an hour. It must be thick to keep well. The flavor will be much improved by boiling in the syrup, half a pint of the kernels cracked. They must be strained out. Plums may be hardened by scalding them in alum water; and when drained, pouring the hot syrup over them every day for a week, but if done with care they will remain whole preserved as above.

EGG PLUMS WHOLE

Take them before they are perfectly ripe, prick them all over with a fork, leave on the stems. To three pounds of plums, allow three pounds and a half of white broken sugar; a half pint of clear hard water; put in your plums and hang over a moderate fire; boil gently and skim. As soon as they begin to crack or shrivel, take them out with a spoon one at a time, and lay them in dishes to cool. Smooth the skins down with your fingers if broken or ruffled. Lay them, when cold, in the syrup, which should be slowly boiling, and let them simmer till they are clear, but not till they break. Put them up in jars.

CITRONS

They should not be too ripe. Cut the soft part out, and let them lie in cold water all night. Boil them very tender, drain them on a cloth, and to every three pounds of citron add four pounds of sugar, two quarts of water, and two ounces of ginger; boil them for half an hour. The next day, boil them till very clear, take them out, and add one pound more sugar, moistened with a little water and the juice of five or six lemons; boil it a few minutes, put the citron in jars, pour the syrup over them, and, when cold, tie down very close.

APPLES

These make as nice a sweetmeat as any other fruit. They may be done whole by paring them. Boil them in just enough water to cover them, half an hour slowly. Then pour the apple water on the sugar, and boil till clear and thick, skimming it carefully; if you add lemons, have them ready, and lay in with the apples, and let them boil till the apples are tender and clear, but not till they break. When cold, put them in jars. They look well cut in halves; preserved with lemons or oranges, or alone, with a little of the essence or oil of lemon. If in halves or quarters, boil in the syrup till clear.

CRAB APPLES

These should be ripe; simmer them till the skins come off easily; take them out; peel and core them with a small knife, and try not to break them. Allow a pound and a half of sugar to a pound of fruit and half a pint of water. When hot and skimmed, lay them in and boil until clear and tender. Spread them on dishes to cool, then place them in jars, and pour the liquor over. Some think their flavor improved by lemon peel boiled with them.

PINE APPLES

Take those that are ripe and fresh; pare off the rind, and cut in slices half an inch thick. Sprinkle between them powdered loaf sugar; and let them remain till the next day. Then with the usual syrup, boil until tender, putting them in when it is cold. Keep in a cool place.

CITRONS AND WATERMELON RINDS

To preserve their greenness, boil them with a layer of vine leaves between each layer of watermelon rinds, pound, and cut in pieces, with water enough to cover. Some add a few pieces of alum. Boil two hours with a thick cloth, or a plate to fit in, over them. Spread on a dish to cool. Then boil in a syrup two hours with the juice and rind of one lemon. Lay the rind in jars and cover.

WHOLE STRAWBERRIES

Take some of the largest and best kind; have ready some boiling syrup, in a large preserving pan; put them in gently, let them boil five minutes. The next day, strain the syrup from them and boil it, and pour it over them. Continue to do so until the thin syrup has done rising; then put them in jars. Tie them down securely.

TO PRESERVE GREEN GAGES

They should be gathered when quite dry and not too ripe. Put them in a preserving pan, with a layer of vine leaves under and over; cover with water, a small piece of alum, and the same of saltpeter. Simmer them very gently till green and tender; take them out carefully into a pan of cold water, drain them in a cloth, and have ready a thin syrup to put them in. Boil the syrup every day, adding a little sugar, till of a proper thickness; the last day, put the gages in and boil for a few minutes.

PUMPKIN

Cut it in pieces of two inches in breadth and four in length. Soak it in lemon juice and sugar, or vinegar, over night. Next day prepare a syrup and lay in the pieces and juice; and boil slowly until tender and transparent, but not long enough to break or lose its form. Boil lemon parings, cut in strips, with it. Spread the pieces to cool. Strain the syrup, and put up in glass jars.

OIL OF PUMPKIN SEED

One gallon of seed will give about half a gallon of lamp oil, and it may be used as olive oil. It is pressed like flaxseed.

APRICOTS

Take those that are ripe; scald, peel, and cut in half, and extract the stones. Put them in layers with sugar between, in a tureen or dish, and let them stand all night. Boil in a syrup a quarter of an hour, and spread to cool. Then boil again in the same syrup, and put away in jars.

MARMALADES

They may be made of any fruit without seeds. The fruit should be boiled very soft with some of the kernels; and all of the pits of quinces and parings, boiled and strained, added to the sugar. Mash to a fine pulp, and add sugar in the proportions of the sweetmeats, and simmer thick. It should be a smooth thick mass. Put up in tumblers.

JELLIES

Almost all kinds of fruit will make a nice jelly. Plums, cherries, currants, grapes, quinces, peaches, apples, oranges are all delicate and very nice. They should be boiled in considerable water very tender, with the seeds and parts of the kernels. Then strain through a jelly bag, and allow a pound of sugar to a pint of juice. Boil a while; if boiled too long, it will not form. Isinglass may be added if there is a failure, which will be a remedy.

APPLE JELLY

Take a peck of nice, juicy apples; pare and core them. Put them into a pan with two quarts of water; boil them gently, but not too much; strain the juice through a bag or sieve; to every pint add three quarters of a pound of loaf sugar and the rind of a lemon pared very thin. Boil it twenty minutes or half an hour.

CHERRY JAM

Take twelve pounds of good, juicy cherries, stone and mash them as much as possible, put them in a pan, and let them simmer gently till the juice is nearly dried up. Add three pounds of finely powdered sugar and the kernels; stir it all well together, and boil till it will drop off the spoon. This should be put in saucers or shallow jars.

RASPBERRY JAM

To each pound of fruit, allow three quarters of a pound of fine loaf sugar. Mash the berries and break the sugar. Mix together, boil, stir, and skim; the jam will be done in half an hour. Put it warm in glasses, and tie up with papers over the top. Other jams are made in the same way.

MORE JAM

Take half a gallon of the greenest apples, pare and core them, put them in a pan with water to cover them, boil one hour, strain the juice, and to every pint add three quarters of a pound of sugar, the juice of two lemons, and the rind of one. Boil one hour.

TO DRY CHERRIES AND PLUMS

Stone them, and half dry them. Pack them in jars, strewing sugar between each layer. They are very nice in pies, and otherwise.

DRIED CHERRIES

Stone them, and to every pound of fruit take half a pound of sugar; put the cherries in an earthen pan, a layer of fruit, and a layer of sugar; let them stand three days, then boil them a few

minutes. When cool, take them out of the syrup and drain them, spread them thin on hair sieves, and dry them in the sun. They should be turned every few hours, on clean sieves till dry.

APPLE BUTTER

Take any kind of berries or other fruit. Allow half a pound of sugar to a pound of fruit; boil till reduced one fourth. nice for children instead of butter.

BUTTER

Keep your pails, churn, and pans sweet. In winter, warm the pans and churns with hot water; in summer, cool them with cold. Keep your milk in summer where it is cool and airy, in winter where it is warm. In warm weather skim your milk as soon as it is thick; in colder weather skim as soon as there is a good thick cream, and be careful not to let it remain too long, as it will acquire a bad taste. Churn as often as you have cream enough, never less than once a week. If the cream is of the right temperature when commenced, it will not froth, and if it does, put in a little salt. Use no salt but the best ground salt. Work out all the butter milk with a ladle in summer, in winter use clean hands. If you wish to keep it some time, put it down in a jar or firkin, or pickle in layers, as clean and free from buttermilk as it is possible, leaving a space for pickle over it, in the following proportions. Half a pail of water, one quart of fine salt, two ounces of loaf sugar, one ounce of saltpeter, well boiled and skimmed. When cold, cover with this, and it will keep good and sweet the year round.

TO MAKE YELLOW BUTTER IN WINTER

Just before the termination of churning, put in the yolk of eggs. It has been kept a secret, but its value requires publicity.

FROSTED FRUIT

Beat the whites of eggs and dip in the fruit; then lay it in finely powdered sugar; lay them on a pan with white paper under, and set them in an oven nearly cool to dry. When the icing is firm, pile them on a dish and set in a cool place.

TO KEEP APPLES FRESH A YEAR

Dry sand and dry your barrel. Put in a layer of apples, and a layer of sand, and so on until full; cover it tight; and keep where they will not freeze in winter. They will be fair and fine flavored the next summer.

TO KEEP GRAPES, PLUMS, ETC., THROUGH THE WINTER

Put them in layers of cotton, until your jar is full; cover close, and keep from frost. It is said they will keep immersed in molasses.

ITALIAN MODE OF PRESERVING STRAWBERRIES

Place as many berries as will form a layer at the bottom of the dish, and sprinkle on powdered loaf sugar; then another layer and sugar again. When your dish is sufficiently full, squeeze over them the juice of a fresh lemon; stir them round before serving, that they may imbibe the lemon and sugar. They are said to be truly delicious.

STRAWBERRIES FOR TEA

They should have nearly their weight in sugar, and a sweet rich cream, to serve with them, and there is no greater luxury.

PEACHES FOR TEA

They should be pared and cut in slices and covered with sugar and sweet cream.

PEARS FOR TEA

Very ripe soft pears, may be prepared like peaches and are very nice.

Blueberries, raspberries, currants, and whortleberries should be used like strawberries.

TOMATOE FIGS

Take six pounds of sugar to one peck or sixteen pounds of the fruit. Scald and remove the skin of the fruit in the usual way. Cook them over a fire, their own juice being sufficient, with the addition of water, until the sugar penetrates and they are clarified. They are then taken out, spread on dishes, flattened, and dried in the sun. A small quantity of the syrup should be occasionally sprinkled over them while drying, after which, pack them down in boxes, treating each layer with powdered sugar. The syrup is afterwards concentrated and bottled for use. They keep well from year to year, and retain surprisingly their flavor, which is nearly that of the best quality of fresh figs. The pear shaped, or single tomatoes, answer the purpose best. Ordinary brown sugar may be used, a large portion of which is retained in the syrup.

ORANGE SYRUP

This syrup is so easily made, and can be used so constantly with advantage, that no housekeeper should be without it. Select ripe and thin-skinned fruit, squeeze the juice through a sieve; to every pint, add a pound and a half of powdered sugar; boil it slowly, and skim as long as any scum rises; you may then take it off, let it grow cold, and bottle it off. Be sure to secure the corks well. Two tablespoons of this syrup, mixed in melted butter, make an admirable sauce for a plum or batter pudding; it imparts a fine flavor to custards, and a teaspoon introduced into a glass of punch adds much to its deliciousness.

ORANGE MARMALADE

Take three dozen Seville oranges, grate the rind off eight, peel the remainder, and throw the rinds in cold water; wash them well, and boil them till tender; divide the oranges, and scrape out all the pulp, but be careful not to have any of the seeds among it; cut  the rinds in thin strips, and add them to the pulp and that which is grated. Weigh it, and to every pound of fruit add one pound and a quarter of sugar. Boil it quickly for twenty minutes.

SEVILLE ORANGES OR LEMONS IN SYRUP

Choose those that are clear and free from spots; wipe them, and let them remain in water a day and night; boil them till tender; drain them, and make a thin syrup, sufficient to cover them, in which they need to boil for a quarter of an hour. Repeat this every day, until the syrup is a proper thickness. Put them into jars, and tie them close down.

REGULATIONS FOR A DINNER TABLE

Let the cloth be laid on accurately, observing to have the middle fold exactly through the center of the table. When even, lay the plates, one at each end and around the sides at equal distances from each other. Lay the napkins neatly folded near each plate. Place the knives and forks that the ends of the handles come even with the edge of the table, the blade towards the plate. The carving knives and forks at each end and by those dishes that are to be carved

Then place your tumblers about three inches from the edge of the table at the right side of the plate. Your table spoons, as many as are needed, may be crossed and laid each side of the carver's plate. Let the castor be well filled and clean and placed in the center. The salt stand well filled; the spoons perfectly bright and placed at convenient distances for use. Let there be nothing wanting that may be needed on the table.

FOR PLACING THE MEATS AND VEGETABLES

Soup or fish should always be set at the head of the table. Or if you have boiled and roasted meats, place the boiled meat at the head. The principal dishes go at the head, and if there are one or two smaller ones, place them opposite to each other at the foot

If there are four, place the two smallest at the sides. If there are five, put the smallest in the middle, and the other four opposite each other at the head, foot, and sides, and so on.

The vegetables should be placed in a straight line at the sides. A middling dinner well served up, the dishes placed at proper distances, and well matched, has a more pleasing aspect, and is more acceptable

than double the quantity crowded and in confusion. Great attention should be paid to these rules.

FOR SERVING A DINNER

When everything is in perfect readiness, and the chairs are placed round the table, open the door and announce dinner in a pleasant kind tone. When the company rise to go out, stand by the door holding it open until they have all passed through, then shut the door and follow to the dining room. If there are covers, remove them as soon as the company are seated. Take them off with the left hand turning them up quick that no water may drop from them. Put them on a side table, to be taken from the room when convenient. Always go to the left hand when you are serving those at table, except to pour water, that should be done at the right. Be attentive to the wants of those at table. Notice if each one is well helped, and be ready to hand anything that is wanted. Do not wait to be asked for everything by the company. If you keep a sharp eye on the table you will see many things wanted that is not asked for, such as bread, vegetables, sauce, etc. As soon as you perceive the signal to remove the first course, take a knife tray and remove all the knives, forks, spoons and ladles from the sauce boats first, then the plates. Begin at the bottom dish on the left side, and take all before you as you proceed until you come to the bottom again. When all is cleared away, take a fork and plate and take up all the pieces of bread from the cloth. Then take another plate and table-brush or a clean towel rolled up, and begin at the bottom on the left side, brushing off clean all the crumbs round the table. If there are finger glasses to be used place them half filled with water at the right side of each person. Put on the piles of plates at the head and foot according to the dishes requiring them. Place the pies at each end, custard and puddings at the sides, with a knife and fork on each pie, and spoons for the side dishes. Place the cheese in the center, if in a tray; if there are two, one at each end.

Putting on the dessert. If the cloth is to be removed before serving the dessert, first take off the finger glasses, beginning at the bottom, then the plates, dishes, etc. in the same order as before; then the napkins and cloth. Then take a towel and wipe off the table, and proceed to put round the plates. If you have cake, place that in the center, the others in a straight line, the sugar basin and water pitcher between. If you have side dishes, place them at equal distances to match in size and color as near as possible. When you have all your dishes on the table, put a knife to your cake, and half a dozen large spoons to serve the dessert with. When there is blanc mange or ice cream, lay a small pile of plates at the top and bottom, and when all are served, then proceed to take all the dirty things from the room with as little noise as possible. In serving a table it should be done with a light quick step, but never with bustle or hurry. Never seem impatient to leave the room, but quietly wait, and be kindly attentive.

A FEW GENERAL DIRECTIONS FOR CARVING, ETC.

The heads of fish and fowl, pigs, hares, etc. should be placed at the left hand of the carver. The thick end of joints also. If the platter has a place for gravy in one end place it that it may come to the right hand. This should be done when the meats are brought to the table, that they need not be turned. The carving knife should be in good order, with a keen edge. In using it no great strength is required. Practice will render it easy to carve the most difficult articles. It is well to notice how a good carver proceeds when a joint or fowl is before him. The fleshy joints are to be cut in smooth slices, and common carving is needed where the fat and lean are combined. The knife should be passed round the bone in cutting a joint, and great attention should be paid in helping every person to a portion of the best part. The outside piece should be first taken off, in such pieces as have an outside. The question should then be asked which is preferred. Always cut the slices rather thin with a portion of fat with each slice. If there is dressing or stuffing, observe to lay a portion with the meat on each plate. A sirloin may be cut at the end or into the middle. The joints in a loin of mutton or veal, should be divided by the butcher, and then they will be easily carved, and fine slices taken off between the bones. If there are different kinds of meat in piece, ask which will be preferred.

In carving large fowls, place the fork in the breast firmly, and carve first from one side of the breast, taking off the wing and leg, then on the other side, in the same manner, leaving the carcase containing the dressing; ask which part is preferred. Pigeons should be cut in halves either lengthwise or across, and half helped to each person. The skewers should be taken out before the dishes are placed on the table.

To carve a pig. This is generally divided by the cook before it is sent up. First divide the shoulder from the body on one side, and then the leg. The ribs are next to be separated in two or three parts. In serving, some like the ear and jaw, a bit of either with the stuffing should be served with some of the best parts of the pig on each plate.

Rabbits. These are carved by separating the legs and shoulders from the body; the back is divided in two or three parts, cutting through the body; the head may be given to anyone who prefers it, the ears being removed before it is served up.

A saddle of mutton or venison. Commence near the end and carve out lengthwise pieces from the sides of the back bone, a portion of fat to each slice; they should be cut thin and smooth.

Ham should be carved about one-third from the thinnest end, cutting long thin slices.

Spare rib should be cut first from the thick meat, near the back bone, slicing it from the outside. If any prefer the rib bone, they are easily cut through and jointed after the meat is first cut off at the back.

A boiled tongue should be carved through the thickest part, or nearly through the middle; slices from this part are more juicy and tender than from the end. This to accompany any of the white meats is very nice and should be served to any who take chicken, veal, or turkey.

Half a calf's head boiled is a genteel dish, if a small one, and well dressed. When first cut, it should be along the cheek bone in the fleshy part, where many handsome slices may be cut. The throat sweetbread lies at the end of the jaw bone; this may be cut in slices, and the eye cut from the socket. If two are to be obliged, divide it, as some are very fond of the eye, also the palate. There is some gristly fat to be pared off about the ear, and also some good meat to be met with on the under side covering the under jaw.

A cod's head and shoulders, if large and in season, is a very genteel and handsome dish if well boiled. When cut it should be done with a spoon or fish trowel. All the parts are served except the green jelly of the eye, this is never given to anyone. The palate, the tongue, the sound, and jelly about the head are considered very delicate and nice, and should be served with a piece of the fish on each plate.

SERVING TEA

When the tea is to be sent around, let everything be well arranged and in perfect readiness. There should be two at least whose services will be actively required in carrying the waiters. While the tea is pouring, the youngest should take the tea-plates on a small salver and pass them, beginning at the ladies and helping them first; then the gentlemen. As soon as this done, the tea should be brought. The tea-tray should be large, and if coffee is served, place a cup of tea between every two of coffee the first time round as there is generally more coffee taken than tea. One should follow with the cream and sugar, the handles of the sugar-tongs and cream-spoon towards the company. When you first enter the room, cast an eye around the room and observe where the most of the elderly ladies are seated, and proceed forward and help one of them first; lower the waiter that it may be easy to take the tea. Have in another tray, your biscuit spread, wafers, toast, cake, tongue, beef, or whatever is prepared to send, all neatly arranged, to take round as soon as you have served the tea; and if the party is large, this tray should be carried by another while you are serving the tea. When the ladies are all served, then proceed to help the gentlemen, beginning as with the ladies. When all the company are served with the first round, carry out your tray, and

wipe it clean if wet; then take another waiter to receive the cups as soon as needed. During this interval, hand round your cake, &c. etc. When you have received all your empty cups, rinse them, and proceed to serve round another course, beginning at the same lady, and going all round, leaving the lady of the family until the last, as strangers must be served first. This second round is generally enough; but hand round the cake, etc. once or twice after, then carry all out of the room; and if cold weather, see that all the fires burn well.

A FEW OBSERVATIONS TO COOKS

Let your character be remarkable for industry and moderation; your manners and deportment for modesty and humility. Let your dress be distinguished for neatness, avoiding everything that looks like finery.

Never think any part of your business too trifling to be well done. Eagerly embrace every opportunity of learning anything which may be beneficial to yourself or that may benefit others.

Do not throw yourself out of employment for a slight offence, you may repent of it when it is too late. Come when you are called, and do whatever is required cheerfully. Do everything at its proper time. Keep everything in its proper place. Use everything for its proper purpose.

Saucy answers are highly aggravating, and serve no good purpose. Muttering on leaving the room, or slamming the door after you, is as bad as an impertinent reply. It often leads to unhappy consequences; at any rate, you lose the esteem of those who would be your best friends. The indulgence of a bad temper will seriously injure the reputation of those even who are most skilled in your art. "Temper is everything"; this must be carefully cultivated by those who would be useful, or desire to please.

Apply to your employers and ascertain how they like their victuals dressed, whether much or little done. What complexions they wish their roasts, whether light or well browned, or if they like them frothed. How they like their soups and sauces, and what accompaniments they prefer. What flavors they fancy, especially of spices and herbs.

Enter into all their plans of economy, and endeavor to make the most of everything, as well for your own honor, as well as the profit of your employer. Take care that the meat that is to appear again on the table is handsomely cut with a sharp knife, and put on a clean dish. Take care of the gravy left, it will make sauce for other dishes. Many things may be redressed to advantage. The best way to warm cold meat is to sprinkle a little salt over it, and let it warm gradually in an oven. Watch it carefully and turn it often for about an hour. Serve it up with gravy, as if freshly cooked. It is better than hashing it, and if done nicely, the cook will get great credit. Take care of the gravy you have boiled poultry and meat in. You may convert it into the best of soups with the usual seasonings, and make an excellent dish with little expense or trouble. Your soups should be otherwise made of the trimmings of meat, and the bones where the meat has been cut off for other purposes, seasoned with carrots, onions, and herbs, will invariably furnish a rich and palatable dish. To excite the good opinion of the eye is the first step towards awaking a good appetite. Each dish must be well cooked and sent to the table with its proper accompaniment in the neatest and most elegant manner. Decoration is most rationally employed in making a plain nutritious dish inviting. Be careful that nothing is over nor under done. Have everything convenient for use that no time be wasted in looking for things. It is a good plan to keep your peppers, spice, cinnamon, cloves ground, put up in bottles, labeled and corked, that you may have them always ready for immediate use. Have your salt, saleratus, browned coffee, starch, etc. in boxes with covers labeled and placed where they can be used conveniently. Have your rice, coffee, pepper, etc. in bags, hanging in their places. Have a good supply of holders ready made on hand, but two is sufficient to have in use at once. Keep them in their place, that they may not be missing when wanted.

Keep all your sauce-pans, kettles, pots, etc. clean, and ready for use. Be careful not to accumulate cold dishes, but have everything used in its time. A hanging safe, in a cool, dry, airy situation, is a suitable place to keep meat and poultry. They are better to be kept awhile, though not to injure. A careful cook will not suffer anything to be lost for the want of attention. The hams and beef will be packed away early, before they can be injured by insects; the pork will be kept under the brine; the cheese protected from whatever may injure it; and everything will have its appropriate care and be done in its proper time, thus securing a good reputation and making your services valuable. If you expect favor, you must make an effort to deserve it. Be fond of obliging and grateful when obliged. Rather do more than is required of you, than less than your duty. Endeavor to promote the comfort and happiness of each member of the family, and at all times be cheerful, patient, and conscientious.

TREATMENT OF DOMESTICS

She that looks well to the "ways of her household" will consider with kindness each member that constitutes her family. If she has a woman's heart, she will often feel that those whose services she needs, and whose duties are of a toilsome nature, have a claim upon her care and sympathy, and will endeavor to lighten the burden and encourage the hearts of those whose little stock of happiness is so much at her disposal. The kind manner, the approving word, the grateful smile, care for the health and habits that she manifests, soothes the perturbed spirit and has a cheering influence leaving a brighter spot glowing in the bosom. Instruction in what belongs to the duties of their sex, as moral beings, as candidates for immortality, will secure the respect and affection and promote the happiness and well-being of those whose highest aim, and perhaps pleasure, is to make you happy and gain your approbation.

Justice in discharging the smallest obligation is highly important. The wages should be promptly paid, and if you discover an effort to please and regard to your interest, let it not be forgotten, but show your approbation and encourage a continuation of such a desirable course by occasionally rewarding it with some trifle, which is a kind of testimony that will be valued and appreciated. An American female writer has observed that "'scolding has long been considered as ungenteel, and that finding fault in a severe and pettish tone never does any good, that it is the last way to make one sorry for omission or faults." Give reproof in a calm undisturbed manner by first making inquiry, that there may be room for explanation. This is the best discipline to your own feelings, and may save you inflicting wounds that cannot be healed. Better dismiss from your family one that will not conform to its rules, than to have its peace destroyed by unpleasant occurrences.

Chapter 8: WITH ATTENTION TO THE EXTERIOR

GARDEN SHRUBS, FLOWERS, ETC.

Let every home if possible be accompanied with the pleasures and the business of a well " kept" garden. It greatly enhances the delights that cluster there, by furnishing its rich and varied sources for enjoyment. The climbing vine, the swelling bud, the opening blossom, the glowing beauties of Nature's coloring, cannot fail to remind us of the goodness of their Author, and to stir the heart with the most pleasing sensations. How the purple plum, the delicious grape, the fragrant strawberry, and all the tempting fruits and delicacies that hang on every stem mirror to our hearts a picture of Paradise, and

make us feel how sad a curse to be driven at once both from the smiles of the Creator and from the delights of the earthly Paradise, the garden of Eden. Cultivate flowers; it is a healthy employment,

and exhibits evidence of refinement and taste. If you inhabit a cottage, the vines twined at the windows, the sweet-brier by the door, the lilacs down the walk, and the snow-ball here and there will make that cottage-home a place of enchantment. It is flowers that give, even to the log cabin, the appearance of happiness and peace. They draw out our hearts in admiration like the virtues, when connected with deformity, and we cannot avoid yielding the homage of our love.

PRACTICAL HINTS

Shrubs require an annual pruning, to remove the superfluous branches and to form a handsome bush. Apply props to such as need support. Some shrubs may be raised from seed sown in early spring, but they are most commonly obtained from layers, suckers, and cuttings, buds or scions. They require a good soil, and those most tender need protection in winter by a covering of straw, leaves, or litter. To obtain shrubs from slips, it must be done before the buds begin to swell or before they leaf. They should be taken from the parent stem so as to leave an eye or bud at the lower end, and that part should be well covered with earth and the ground kept moist.

GRAPE VINES FOR BEES

It is said to be the most convenient and best thing for bees to alight on when they swarm, and should be always planted near them for that purpose.

BEES

In winter the best place in which to keep bees is a dry, cold, and dark room or outhouse. The colder the winter the better if the air is dry. Damp is injurious and will cause mold in the comb and among the bees.

BEESWAX

Tie it up in a linen or woolen bag with a pebble or two to keep it from floating; place it in a kettle of cola water and place over the fire, as the wax melts it rises to the surface, while all the impurities remain in the bag.

OIL OF FLOWERS

Split cotton wadding and dip in pure Florence or sweet oil; lay this in a jar or china dish, cover it with a thick layer of rose leaves, or any odoriferous flower or plant, from which you wish perfume. Then lay over another layer of cotton steeped in oil, and so on until filled. Cover it closely and place in the sun a week. Throw away the leaves and squeeze the oil in vials for use. The scented cotton will perfume your clothes.

THE BENEFIT OF TOADS

Never destroy them; keep them in your garden to destroy bugs and fleas. They will do more to preserve a garden than a man from insects.

RED RASPBERRY LEAVES

It is asserted that the fine green leaves of the red raspberry gathered in a fair day, and cured in an open room, are not inferior to the China teas.

CUTTINGS OR SLIPS

They should be of the last year's growth, the joints near together, and should be three or four in a cutting. They should be planted from four to six inches from the end of the stem. They should be sheltered, and the ground enriched and loosened. Press the earth around the stem, and insert them about one-third their length. Water them in dry weather, and by autumn they will be rooted.

SUCKERS

These are young plants that shoot up around a shrub or tree from the root; they may be carefully separated in spring or autumn, and transplanted.

LOCUSTS

Sow the seed in March, April, or May, in good sandy loam, half an inch deep. Pour scalding hot water on the seed, and let it stand all night. Pick out such seeds as have swelled, and plant them. Repeat the process with those that did not swell, and sow them, and they will come up the next month abundantly. The next year transplant them into rich sandy ground. They sucker freely, and may be propagated rapidly by transplanting them. Let none be lost.

SHRUBS

There are several varieties of lilacs. And they might be found more abundant than they are. It is not understood how easily, with proper knowledge and suitable care, every dwelling might be furnished with all the common varieties of flowering shrubs. By slips or suckers, the lilac, snowberry, syringa, guilder rose or snowball, laburnum, and others, with their beauty and fragrance, might be made to contribute to our enjoyment, and adorn every "home" in our land.

DAHLIAS

This splendid plant is raised better from the root than from seed. As soon as they have done flowering, the tops should be cut down and the root well covered with litter and earth, to ripen without being injured by frost. In about a week or on appearance of severe weather, they should be dug up and put in dry sand out of the reach of frost. They should neither be kept too damp or dried to a husk. If kept well, they will begin to sprout around the old stem and tubers in March or April. They should then be put in light earth, or in pots, and kept in a warm room and watered. As soon as they have grown two or three inches, they may be divided in such a manner as that each sprout

should have a piece of the tuber strongly attached. Each of these will make a plant, and must be kept growing in separate pots until about the middle of May. Then they may be set out in beds well prepared with compost, and made mellow with the earth they are in around them. When set out, place a neat stake near, that the brittle stem as it grows may be fastened at every joint with twine, as the wind and rain will destroy them. If raised from seed, sow it the last of February or first of March in pots. The earth should be a mixture of sand, leaf mold and compost, or that which is equivalent.

CALLAS OR ETHIOPIAN LILLY

This elegant plant needs moist ground, but should not be watered much while in bud or blossom. It should have plenty of air and light, but too much heat causes it to turn yellow, and its rich leaves to die and fall. This plant is best propagated by suckers, which spring up around the parent stalk.

GERANIUMS

These are propagated easily by slips, placed in pots, and kept from the sun with the ground kept moist. They should not be wet when in full bloom, but it may be done before the buds are expanded.

MONTHLY ROSES

These need sun and air when they are rooted and should be watered in proportion as they receive it. The young wood furnishes buds and blossoms.

THE PASSION FLOWER

This is a beautiful vine and requires to be well trained and supported. They will grow to cover a large surface if properly attended. They must have the climate of a warm room or greenhouse.

THE HONEY SUCKLE

This in its varieties is a desirable vine for the frame work at the door, the piazza, etc. It may be increased by turning the ends downward into the ground. It should be carefully trained.

GARDEN ROSES

These should be pruned after they have done flowering. Cut out the old wood where it is too thick, shorten such shoots as have a good eye or bud and a healthy leaf, and all that grows after this pruning will produce large flowers the next year.

In November cover flowerbeds with leaves, straw, and litter, also the roots of grape vines, and other tender plants and shrubs.

If plants are watered too much, they will perish of mildew. Slips should be exposed gradually to the sun. A piece of the older wood on a cutting causes it to strike root more readily. To avoid the bad effects of evaporation, the leaves are often removed from the lower part of the cutting of shrubs and trees, they are more likely to live and thrive. Take them from branches that grow near the ground.

Transplantation is best done in the spring or fall, but may take place at all seasons, if the newly formed extremities of the root are uninjured.

All garden soil should be dug and made mellow. If insects prevail on plants, they should be fumigated with tobacco, or watered where tobacco leaves have been soaked. April is the time to clip the edgings of box and remove the roots that are superfluous, in a border or on beds. There may be from your yard enough spared to adorn that of a friend. See to it that nothing of the kind is lost. Trim the cuttings of trees or shrubs a little, that the leaves or branches do not touch the ground—it will cause decay. Both ends of a tubular stalk may be inserted in the earth, and it will produce two plants and be most likely to live. Never water the top or leaves of a plant when the sun shines, it should be confined to the root. The watering of plants is best done morning and evening, except when newly transplanted or when shaded from the sun. In September, prepare beds for planting tulips, hyacinths, anemones, ranunculusses, and other flower roots aud shrubs that are to be planted the next month. When necessary trim pines, firs, walnut trees, and maples, as the sap will not so much exude as in spring; also, plant beds of strawberries.

THE SUNFLOWER

One hundred pounds of this seed afford forty pounds of oil. The refuse of the seed after being expressed is good food for animals. The leaves make cigars that are used in medicine; the stalk affords a superior alkali, and the comb of the seed is choice food for swine.

TO OBTAIN DIFFERENT FLOWERS FROM THE SAME STEM

Split a small twig of elderbush lengthwise, and having scooped out the pith, fill each compartment with flower seeds of different sorts but that blossom about the same time. Surround them with mold, and then tying together the two halves, plant the whole in earth. The stems will exhibit to the eye flowers of the different varieties of seed, as from one stem.

TO EXTRACT ESSENTIAL OIL FROM FLOWERS

Take any flowers you like, and lay a layer of flower and then one of salt in an earthen jar, when filled carry it to the cellar; forty days after, strain the whole by pressure. Bottle that essence and expose it four or five weeks in the sun and dew to purify. One drop will scent a quart.

FRUIT TREES

We hear complaints of the decay and death of fruit trees, but it is through neglect or a want of knowlege of their diseases.

SOAP FOR KILLING BORERS IN TREES

Hard soap rubbed carefully into every place in the tree that seems to be wounded by them will destroy effectually these nuisances to gardens and orchards. The rain will dissolve it and force them out of their holes and cause their death. Strong ley put on with a swab or brush is equally good; made of potash, one pound to a gallon of water.

APPLE

Pruning the decayed limbs, rubbing the trunks with a hard brush, and painting with a mixture of soft soap and flour of sulphur, in proportion of five gallons of the former to one of the latter, and also strewing lime under the trees and around the trunks, will prevent decay—revive and almost resusciate the dying. It improves the quality of the fruit, and the grass, and helps to destroy the worms.

PEACH

These trees do best in elevated situations; when the soil is unfavorable on hills, it should be improved ; cold, wet, or spongy soil is unfavorable. When peach trees begin to languish, remove the soil around them, and supply its place with charcoal; it will produce a sudden renovation and improve the richness of the fruit. Prune in the extremities of the branches of bearing trees, two feet in July every year. This will keep the tree full of bearing buds and healthy wood. All trees that have the yellows must be removed as the disease is contagious. Graft them in September. Peach trees may be preserved from the ravages of the worms, by freeing the diseased part from earth and gum, spreading over it a thin coat of common hard soap, and filling up with fresh soil. It not only destroys the insect, but preserves the tree in a healthy state; even if used freely, it will not injure it. Soft soap is equally good applied in the early part of April, and then again in the early part of June. It must be repeated every season, and as it is dissolved by the rain, it descends to the roots, and causes it to grow vigorously, besides destroying insects and eggs, and cleansing the bark. Several hundred trees may be done in a few hours. It is equally good for other fruit.

QUINCE

This is a beautiful tree when in blossom, and when the fruit is ripe, it is highly ornamental. It is easily raised from cuttings or layers taken from the tree in April, and planted in a shady place, and the soil enriched, which will keep it from sudden drought. Also water occasionally. They might grow in any part of the country with suitable care.

PEAR

This tree dies of a disease called the tire blight. It occurs in summer; the leaves from the extremities of the branches, for two or more feet, appear as if scorched. This should be cut off a foot or more from the diseased part, and immediately buried. When this is practised, the evil is arrested.

PLUM

This tree is becoming deplorably affected with the " black gam" caused by an insect. That part where this disease is found should be cut off and burned, without delay. This will preserve it.

THE BEECH TREE

It is said that this tree is never struck by lightning. It has been noticed in Europe and America. Preserve and rear them for the protection of animals on your plantation.

GOOSEBERRY

The bush should not stand against a fence; it should be well
trimmed every spring, especially in the middle of the bush; never
allow two branches to rub against each other. Dig well around it, and
enrich the soil at the time of pruning. Sprinkle them with soap suds
from the washtub three or four weeks before blossoming out; it will
prevent mildew, and produce fine large berries.

RASPBERRY

Set them in cool deep moist soil, in a sheltered and partly shaded
place, and they will throw up suckers to the height of six or eight
feet, and produce large and well-flavored berries.
They are easily cultivated, and rapidly propagated
by cuttings, suckers, and layers. No one who has
enjoyed the luxury of the white raspberry in its
season will be willing to do without them.

CURRANT

Keep the bushes well trimmed, and the fruit
will be much larger and better flavored.

STRAWBERRY

Plant them about two feet apart each way, and cut off the runners, that you may have larger and better fruit, as the sun and air will then more easily circulate through them. Water them around the root, as it spoils the flavor of the fruit to be over-watered. Charcoal dust, and soot, greatly improves the soil of strawberry beds; the soot should be sprinkled, and hoed in during the month of April; and the charcoal after rains, when the ground has become hard.

TOMATO

It is a good plan to sow the seed in a hot-bed, or in boxes, in April, and transplant them when danger from frost is passed. They should be four feet apart in good rich ground, and the vines supported by a framework of some kind, or brush, as the fruit will be better than if left on the ground. The cherry or plum tomato for pickling, and the large red, are best for preserving. Though both are used for a vegetable.

VEGETABLE PLANTS

CELERY

Set out the plants in rich compost and earth six inches apart, as they progress in growth; draw the earth around them, but not to touch the central part; water with salt and water, or scatter salt around the plant, and it will be greatly improved. It is a saline plant, and is found in some countries in ditches near the sea. It may be kept in the cellar or green-house through the winter, for use.

ASPARAGUS

In spring, the soil should be always enriched if not done in the fall, which is preferable. As soon as the frost is out of the ground, the earth should be chopped two or three inches over the beds, and the compost hoed in. Then the toil should be stirred every day or two, to keep out weeds, until the plant comes up. When you cut the tops, take them off even with the surface. This plant also is saline, and is benefitted with waterings of salt and water.

EGG PLANT

The fruit of this plant is highly esteemed by many. The seed should be sown early, and transplanted into the open ground in early June, two feet apart; care should be taken to protect the young plants from the black flea.

CRESS OR PEPPER GRASS

Is a beautiful salad, alone or with lettuce. Sow in drills, and cut before it comes into rough leaf.

RHUBARB

A few stems cut from the roots, and planted in rich ground four feet apart, will furnish stems enough for a family. No garden should be without it, as the stalk is a luxury made into a pie. The leaves are poison. The stalk of this plant may be used without danger, but the leaf is said to contain oxalic acid, and if cooked as greens occasions vomiting and sometimes death.

CUCUMBER

An improved mode of cultivating this favorite plant is in digging a hole in the earth, filling it with about a peck of leeched ashes, and covering the ashes with a small quantity of earth; then planting the seed on a level with the surface of the ground. This has been tried with great success.

BROCCOLI AND CAULIFLOWER

This plant should be cultivated like the common species of cabbage. It is much nicer grown in rich soil, and the ground kept loose about the root.

VEGETABLE OYSTER

There is no vegetable that the lover of the real oyster would value more than this easily cultivated plant. When once in a garden, they are not soon destroyed. They should have good soil, and be cultivated like other spindle-shaped roots.

NASTURCION

This beautiful plant is valued for its cress-like pod, used as a pickle. They need the support of a frame-work of bush to keep them from the ground.

LETTUCE

If you wish to have early salad of this plant, start it in a hot-bed or boxes, and transplant into your garden, setting them far enough apart to keep the earth loose about the toot, and they will head tender and larger.

CANARY BIRDS

THEIR CHARACTERISTICS, DIRECTIONS FOR REARING, FEEDING, AND NURSING THEM

Canaries are not naturally so delicate as they are thought to be, but become so for want of proper care. They excel most other birds in their good qualities. The sweetness of their song continues most of the year, except the time of molting when they are generally silent, though some in spite of this annual illness do not even then lose their song. Their plumage is delicate and sometimes beautiful, which is displayed in different colors, most commonly in a bright yellow or straw color. They are very docile and will learn a variety of leasing little tricks, such as coming at the call and pronouncing words distinctly. They will also learn airs and keep time like a musician. As to the time of pairing, it generally commences about the middle or latter end of March, or perhaps a better criterion would be when the frosts disappear, and the sun sheds an enlivening warmth. Put the pair you intend to match into a small cage, and although they may at first be quarrelsome, they will soon become reconciled, which will be known by their feeding each other, billing, etc. Feed them at the time with the following. Boil an egg very hard, chop, and grate it fine; add bread crumbled equally fine, a little maw seed, mix this well, and give them a tablespoonful twice a day. In ten days they will be paired. Place the cage in a room that enjoys the morning sun, and not where it shines hot in the afternoon, as the excessive heat will produce sickness, breed mites, etc. Place in the cage a little hay and cow's hair; the latter after serving once may be washed and dried for future use in building nests. The nest boxes are composed of wicker, or wire bottoms, so that the dust falls through, and there should be but one in a cage at a time or until the hen has hatched, then put in another and make the nest for them, as it saves them much fatigue; if it does not please them they will adapt it to their fancy. The following food must be given when they have young: Boil an egg and grate it—take as much bread as the size of an egg and grate and mix well together, and feed them a spoonful three times a day. For a change soak a piece of stale sweet-bread in water—squeeze it out and add a little sweet milk and feed them—also give them a little cabbage in its season. This and chickweed, and salad, may be given in their season three times a day. But if they are given early in the year before the bitterness has passed away they are hurtful. The hen sits thirteen but more generally fourteen days. Clean the perches, fill one fountain with water and the other with seed, so that they shall not be disturbed for two or three days after they hatch. When your young ones can feed themselves, you may cage them off, and give them egg and bread as before stated, with a little maw seed, with some ground or bruised rape, till they are seven weeks old; when they will be able to crack hard seed, which should be given them before that time. If you wish to make one very tame you can bring it up by hand, taking it from the old ones as soon as they are fledged, or feathered, which will be in eleven or twelve days. When taken from the hen, it should be placed in a warm box, and placed in rather a dark situation, to make it forget the old ones.

Sometimes you will be obliged to remove them. If the hen should be ill, they should be taken from her, for she cannot feed them; and when she leaves them to the care of the male bird or if she plucks the feathers from her young, they should be removed, as in that case she will kill them in two or three days.

The following paste may be given, which will keep good fifteen days. Bruise in a mortar or on a table with a rolling pin a quart of rape seed in such a manner that you can blow the chaff away, and a piece of bread, reducing them to powder. Put it in a dry box arid keep it from the sun. Give a teaspoonful of this and a little hard egg grated with a few drops of water. This will become unfit for them after twenty days, as then it will be sour. It may be given without harm to the old birds if necessary, but it must be given dry. Or if preferred, you may give, for the first three days, grated egg and sponge biscuit made fine and mixed with a little water to make it like paste. Then add a small quantity of scalded rape seed, as then they are strong enough to digest it. They may also have a small quantity of chickweed seed, and a sweet almond peeled and chopped fine. The chickweed may be given twice a day in very hot weather.

Birds brought up by hand require to be fed once in two hours. To feed them, sharpen a little stick of wood and give them at each feeding four or five mouthfuls, or until they refuse to open their mouths voluntarily. At a month old you may cease feeding them with a stick, as they will then begin to feed alone. You must put them in a cage without perches first, and have a little bird seed in a box or glass, and in about seven weeks take the soft food by degrees away, and leave only the hard seed. It will be well occasionally to give a little bruised hempseed, especially in winter. If they are ill when young, treat them as follows. Bruise some hempseed and soak it a little in water, then squeeze it through a cloth, which forms what is called the milk of hempseed. This will strengthen and nourish young birds very much, but you must take the water glass away when you give this medicine.

DISEASES TO WHICH THEY ARE SUBJECT

Outward signs are absolutely necessary to judge of their diseases, and when ill they exhibit strong symptoms. The first spoken of, is the swelling of the stomach, which attacks them at a month or six weeks old, in consequence of over feeding on soft food such as salad and chickweed. The extremity of the body becomes swollen, of a dark red colour, and very hard, full of small red veins and the bowels seem to protrude. For this, put in a small piece of alum in the water and renew it every day, for three or four days at least. This will frequently be found to answer. Another remedy is to put a rusty nail into the water, which should be changed twice a week leaving the nail in it. Boiled bread and milk with canary seed boiled in it is sometimes effectual. Put it inside the cage for five or six mornings and at twelve o'clock you may give the usual food. Another remedy is to put the bird in lukewarm milk for six or eight minutes, that a portion of it may be absorbed by the pores, then put him in warm spring water, after which wipe him with a soft muslin before the fire until dry. Then put him in his cage and place it before the fire a short distance or in the hot sun in the room. After putting him in his place give him lettuce seed and let him rest the next day; repeat this on the third day, and if necessary three or four times with the interval of a day each time—as much for the repose of the bird as for the remedy to operate. This gives relief if faithfully applied.

The molt, or renewal of the feathers, is also a dangerous time; it occasions sometimes death. Very few die if the autumn is fine and temperate. It generally attacks young birds when about six weeks old, and lasts two months. They appear melancholy and often sleep in the day with their head under their wing. The cage will be full of small feathers, as young birds do not cast the wing or tail feathers the first year, but the second they molt throughout. At this time they eat but little and only such as they like best, they require a variety of nourishing food and require to be kept warm. The least cold at this time will prove fatal. If they are bad you may give them a piece of sponge cake or biscuit soaked in white wine; sherry is best, if they eat this it will do them much good, and it is good to sprinkle a little over them and place them before the fire. A little refined liquorice in the water is good. A few grits make them cast their feathers while molting. If they should have a small pimple on the extremity of the body and appear rather dull, cut off the top of it with a pair of scissors and put on a little salt and sugar, and if the pimple is not well formed put on sweet oil.

They sometimes have red mites if the cage is not kept clean. It may be discovered by their frequent plucking and feathering themselves. But it may be avoided by cleaning the cage twice a week.

Canaries are subject to other diseases, which may be cured without much trouble. If they are attacked with diarrhea, pull a few feathers out of the tail, and rub on the oil of sweet almonds on the lower part of the body. Give them hard yolk of egg, grated sponge cake, scalded lettuce, and melon seed for food.

If they throw their seed about the cage without eating it is an indication that they need purging. Give them rape seed with a lettuce leaf or a little chickweed seed which will soon relieve.

When paired, the hen is sometimes "eggbound," and falls off the perch on her back, and if not helped dies. For this take her out of the cage and rub on the oil of sweet almonds gently on the lower part of the body which enables them to discharge the egg. A piece of mortar laid in the cage will also relieve. This should be kept in, to prevent this difficulty.

If they break a leg take out the perches and put soft hay at the bottom of the cage, also their food. Their cage should be covered that they may not be disturbed.

Birds in molting sometimes lose their song ; good and flourishing food will restore; put liquorice in the water.

If a bird should have a swelling on the beak or foot wash it with sweet oil or milk—taking care to keep the cage very clean, that no dirt or dust adhere to the sore.

GENERAL DIRECTIONS

To keep canaries healthy, the cage should be washed as often as once in two weeks and often cleaned. Fresh lettuce or cabbage may be given them in July and August, plantain is also good, it may be given in hot weather three times a day. Lettuce seed and plantain seed is also good to be given as food, mixed in a small pot. In hot weather they should have clean water in pans once a day to wash and bathe in, which greatly refreshes them. A piece of cuttlefish bone or sand, should be in the cage to keep them in a healthy condition. Their fountains should be filled, and the water fountains changed every day. The bird seed is a mixture already prepared, to be used as it is. Sponge cake may be given occasionally, but food containing salt is injurious; crackers, sweet apples, and worms are also good.

To distinguish the male from female, it is observed that a streak of bright yellow may be noticed over the eyes and under the throat, his head is wider and longer and in general is much higher colored, his feet too are larger. They also begin to warble first, which is often at a month old. They are quicker, more taper, and sprightlier than the hens. If the hen lays, take out the egg and substitute an ivory or wooden one, as they then will hatch all at the same time. If the hen does not lay before eight o'clock in the morning, she is ill and needs remedies spoken of before.

Canaries may be taught to sing entire tunes by means of a flageolet or bird organ, in the following manner. In ten or twelve days, when he begins to feed himself, take him away from all the other birds, or sooner if he begins to sing. Let his cage be covered with a thin linen cloth eight days; then take the instrument and play one tune five or six times a day for fifteen days, then remove the linen cloth and substitute a green or red one of a thick material. He must remain covered in this way until he is perfect in the air you wish him to learn. During this time it is best to put in his seed at night, that his attention be not divided. The organ should be sweet toned, as they copy with great exactness. Some learn in two, and others in six months. This makes a bird a great favorite and of course valuable.

OTHER BIRDS

TREATMENT OF THE MOCKING BIRD

This is one of the sweetest songsters in the universe; he can imitate the whole grove of melody, and of himself can make a concert; his imitative powers display the Creator's wisdom and goodness in a greater measure than any other bird. He can be made so docile as to perch and sing upon the hand, he never tires in his sweet employment; night and day he warbles incessantly so that the American Nightingale (as he is sometimes called) is like that of which Cowper says,

"Ten thousand warblers cheer the day
And one the live-long night."

The treatment of the mocking bird is net very peculiar or troublesome, only requiring to be fed every morning with Indian meal wet with milk not very stiff. Whortleberries, cedar, elder, and pokeberries may be given to them freely, also wild cherries in the month of October and November may be used. It is a good plan to dry them for winter use; these birds thrive best with a great deal of natural food. An egg boiled hard and grated is good, also a small piece of raw minced beef to be given occasionally. During the summer, air is beneficial, but not the sun. A little water in a cup for washing once a week is of service, but the greatest care is required when molting, which is from August till November. He should be kept from cold draughts of air and well supplied with berries, spiders, and grasshoppers, as they live in their native woods mostly on insects. They should be fed and watered regularly every morning by eight o'clock. When this bird becomes sickly treat him very kindly, give him spiders daily, also meal worms, which may be found in granaries. Put gravel on the bottom of the cage, and keep them quiet.

The male is known from the female by a regular line of white feathers in the wing, which in a fine bird forms almost a curve from the shoulder to the tip of the wing. They are after all difficult to distinguish, as some of the finest birds when young are found to have been irregularly marked. They are not completely plumed until they are two years old. They sing from January until the last of August.

AMERICAN YELLOW BIRD

This bird is very common in the middle states, and partakes much of the nature of the canary. They are of a dark yellow, have dark wings, and have a dark spot on the head. They are admired both for their plumage and their song. If placed near a canary  they will acquire many of its notes. It should be an old established singing canary, otherwise they will take the yellow bird's song to the detriment of his own. They should be fed with yellow and hempseed; two thirds of the former. A leaf of lettuce, cabbage, or a piece of apple is of service. Strew a little brown gravel on the cage.

CAROLINA RED BIRD

This bird is indigenous to the Southern states, and is seldom seen north of Virginia. They are greatly admired for their brilliant plumage, being a fine scarlet with a beautiful topped head. Their notes are free, but not particularly sweet. Being a southern bird they delight in a warm temperature, of which care must be taken in winter. Their natural food is rice. The rough or unhulled rice mixed with hemp seed, which may be found already mixed, should be kept for them. A small quantity of cracked corn is of service. The same directions apply to the Java Sparrow.

THE AMERICAN ROBIN

This bird is not the robin redbreast of Europe, ours is a much larger bird. Their plumage (the male) is a rich hazel colour, with clear white stripes under the throat: the back is of a dark brown, eyes very sharp, of a dark hazel with a delicate outward ring; their carriage is erect and bold, which is pleasing. They can be tamed to come out of their cage at the call of a name; they can be taught to imitate a flute with surprising accuracy. It is related of one that he whistled a tune so correctly that it might have been mistaken for a flute or flageolet. There has been one kept by a gentleman that played on band instruments, and the bird caught the marches, to the astonishment of everyone that heard it. They are treated like the mocking bird.

HOW TO TAKE CARE OF RABBITS

There are several varieties, but the broad chested and short legged are the best. Rabbits require much the same food as sheep and generally the treatment so far as food is concerned. They should be fed three times a day with dry substantial food. The grain best for them is oats, peas, wheat, pollard, or shorts, and some use buckwheat. The greens and roots the same as for cattle and sheep—carrots, Jerusalem artichokes, boiled potatoes, lucerne, clover, cabbage leaves, tares, etc. The best dried herbage is clover, hay, and pea and bean straw.

The utensils used for feeding them should be made of something they cannot destroy, as they are apt to gnaw all wood. They will rear five or six litters in a season, and increase rapidly, as they produce five or six at a time. A warren should be provided for their use with artificial mounds of sand where they can provide themselves sleeping places, etc.

Rabbits are eagerly sought in market. Some of the larger kinds if cooked in the same way are equal in flavour to a turkey and are highly prized. Rabbits are in perfection at the fourth or sixth month, then they become more dry in flesh and somewhat hard. Three months is the time allowed to make a rabbit fat and ripe. For the table or the invalid their flesh is equal to poultry. If they are ever diseased, it is in consequence of too much green food, and may be remedied by using grain and dry food.

THE MANAGEMENT OF HENS

Their habitation in winter should be warm, and if convenient made to come to the ground and supplied with old plastering, ashes, pulverized oyster shells, and charcoal; give them fresh water once or twice a week. Beef's liver or some other kind of meat, baked or boiled potatoes warm, fragments of cooked vegetables, and keeping corn always by them, is the best manner of feeding them, and they thus are always sufficiently fat for the table. It is a good plan to soak their corn, and when they have it always in their trough they take but a few kernels at a time, but when irregularly fed they will eat too much and stop laying, and not unfrequently become diseased.

Hen houses should be kept clean, their roosts also. Broken or bad eggs should not be allowed to remain in the nests, and it is well to have lime or ashes at the bottom under the hay. Dirty water should not be given—their food should be fresh and free from fermentation, and in this way from a flock of a dozen hens a family may have plenty of fresh eggs during the year.

To prevent lice, a mixture of sulphur in their food once a fortnight should be given, and it is also a remedy—it may be given in small quantities to young chickens for the same purpose.

RULES WITH INEVITABLE INTRUSIONS

TO DESTROY CROWS IN CORNFIELDS

Steep corn in arsenic and place where they come, and it is said they will never come again.

THE RED ANT

Where they are troublesome, it is said that sage leaves freshly picked will keep them away if scattered in places you wish to protect.

AN INSECT TRAP

Scoop out the inside of a turnip, scollop the edges, and place it downward on the earth. The insects will pass 'into it as a place of retreat through the holes, and the cucumbers, squashes, melons, etc. may soon be clear of them.

COCKROACHES

Procure from the Druggist a small quantity of poke root, boil in water til the juice is extracted, mingle the liquor with molasses and spread it on large platters or soup plates in places where they visit, and they will be slain by hundreds in the following morning. The root after being boiled, laid in closets, etc. will prevent their troubling you.

TO KILL WEEDS IN GRAVEL AND BRICK WALKS

Keep them moist with brine a week in the spring, and three or four days in the fall, and it will prevent their growing.

A NEW RAT TRAP

Take a smooth kettle, fill to within six inches of the top with water, cover the surface with chaff or bran, place where the rats harbor, and it will drown all that get into it. Thirty-six were taken in one night by this process.

TO PROTECT GRAIN, ETC. FROM RATS

Green elder boughs scattered in and about places where they are troublesome, it is said, will protect effectually against their depredations.

MAD DOGS, A PREVENTIVE

Mix a small portion of the flour of sulphur with their food or drink. This has been known in Europe for centuries and is used to prevent this disease from breaking out among the packs of hounds upon the estates of English noblemen.

GAPES IN CHICKENS

A preventive is said to be vinegar that has stood in iron, to put a little in their food every few days. It is caused by worms in the throat, and it is said there is no effectual remedy better than giving sulphur in their drink, a pepper corn occasionally. They may be reached and taken out of the throat with the end of a feather.

TO DESTROY MOTHS

The vegetable musk seed should be thinly laid in the folds of fir or woolens. These seeds are highly esteemed by French perfumers for their fragrance. To destroy the vitality of the eggs, which produce moths, a weak solution of oxmuriate of mercury in the spirits of rosemary, half drachm to a pint, or a weak solution of arseniate of potash in the same spirit, about fifteen grains to a pin, is employed in preparing birds for stuffing, to prevent their being injured by moths.

TO KEEP AWAY MOSQUITOES

Attach a piece of flannel or sponge to a thread made fast to the top of the bedstead, wet the flannel or sponge with camphorated spirits, and they will leave the room.

TO DESTORY BEDBUGS

Rub the bedsteads well with lamp oil; this alone is good, but to make it more effectual, get a sixpence worth of quicksilver and add to it, put it into all the cracks around the bed and they will soon disappear. The bedsteads should first be scalded, and wiped dry, then put on with a feather.

ANTIDOTE AGAINST MICE

Gather wild mint, put it where you wish to keep them out, and they will not trouble you.

Chapter 9: CHOICE RECEIPTS FOR FABRICS AND SOAPS

DYEING

GENERAL RULES

The materials should be clean, rinsed from soap, and entirely wet, that they may not spot. Light colors should be steeped in brass, tin, or earthen, and if set at all, with alum. Dark colors should be steeped in iron and set with copperas.

FOR SKY BLUE

Get the blue composition. It may be found at the Druggists or Clothiers for a shilling an ounce. If the articles are not white, the old colors should be all discharged by soap or a strong tartaric acid water, then rinsed. Twelve or sixteen drops of the composition stirred into a quart bowl of soft warm water and strained if settlings are seen, will dye a great many articles. If you want a deeper color, add a few drops more of the composition. If you wish to color cotton goods, put in pounded chalk to destroy the acid, which is very destructive to all cotton. Let it stand until the effervescence subsides, and then it may be safely used for cotton as well as silk.

FOR LILAC

Take a little pinch of Archil and put some boiling hot water upon it, add to it a very little lump of pearlash. Shades may be altered by pearlash, common salt, or wine.

A PURPLE SLATE

One paper of ink powder, one quart of vinegar, sufficient water to wet the articles well. Done in brass.

NANKIN COLOR

A pail full of lye with a piece of copperas half as big as a hen's egg boiled in it will produce a nankin color that will not fade.

A COMMON SLATE

Tea grounds boiled in iron and set with copperas will make a good slate. Also birch bark boiled in copper, brass, or tin and set with copperas will produce a fine slate; set with alum a bright nankin color.

LEMON COLOR

Peach leaves, bark scraped from the barberry bush, saffron, etc., steeped in water and set with alum, will color a bright lemon; drop in a little gum Arabic to make the articles stiff.

ROYAL PURPLE

Soak logwood chips in soft water until the strength is out, then add alum, a teaspoon to a quart of the liquor. If this is not bright enough, add more alum. Rinse and dry. When the dye is exhausted, it will color a fine lilac.

CRIMSON PER POUND

One ounce of cream tartar, two ounces of powdered alum, one ounce of cochineal, two drachms of powdered sal ammonia, quarter of an ounce of pearlash, six ounces wheat bran. Take a brass or copper kettle with four gallons of rain water; when at scalding heat, add the cream tartar and alum. Let the liquor boil, then put in the cloth, stirring it frequently for an hour and a half. Take out the cloth, rinse it in cool water, and air it. Empty the dye and put in as much clean soft water as before; when blood warm, add the bran tied in a bag, take off the scum as it rises, while the water heats moderately. Take out the bag, add one ounce of cochineal, boil it, put in the cloth, stir it for an hour, rinse in cold water. Empty the dye, and put in as much clear water as before; when as warm as the hand can bear, put in the sal ammonia; when dissolved put in the cloth, move it hastily for five minutes, and then drain. Now add the pearlash and mix it. When almost scalding hot, put in the cloth and move it constantly for ten minutes. Take it out, air, and rinse it, and the color will be permanent and beautiful.

GREEN PER POUND

If you cannot get the blue composition, or prefer to prepare it, the following is a receipt for making it. Ingredients for the whole: one ounce and a half oil of vitriol, quarter ounce of indigo, one ounce of cream tartar, two ounces alum, eight ounces fustic. Prepare the compound in the following manner. Put the oil of vitriol in a glazed earthen jar, and add the indigo pounded fine and sifted. Stir it hastily with a stick to produce general fermentation. When done add half a tablespoon of water, stir it, and in one day it will be fit for use. If it does not ferment, it is not good. To dye, prepare a brass or copper kettle with three gallons of water per pound of woolen; add the cream tartar and alum when the water is scalding hot. Make it boil. When dissolved, put in the cloth and boil one hour and a half, stirring occasionally. Then take it out, drain, and air it. Put in water enough to make up the deficiency caused by boiling, and add two thirds of the compound, mixing it well. Then put it in again, keeping the dye only at scalding heat, moving it often in the dye. After half an hour take it out, air, and rinse it. Put the fustic in a thin bag, boil it in the liquor an hour and a half. Take out the bag and put in the woolen, boil gently more than an hour, airing it once in the time. If you wish to make a different shade, after airing it, add a little more of the compound or fustic as the case may be. Air and rinse it.

ORANGE PER POUND

One ounce of annatto or otter, two ounces of pearlash. Cut the annatto and put it in a bag, soak it in two and a half gallons of water. Add to the above one ounce of pearlash and boil it one hour. Wet your woolen in hot water, drain it, and put it in the dye. Stir it one hour while it boils. Dry and then rinse.

CINNAMON COLOR

For twenty-four yards of woolen cloth, take three pounds of ground camwood, three pecks of butternut bark. Put your water in a brass or iron kettle, and let it boil a few minutes to extract the strength. Put in your cloth, stirring it often, and let it boil an hour or more. Then take it out and air it. Put it in the same length of time, and air it as before. If the color is not dark enough, dissolve a little copperas in hot water, and add to the dye. Boil the cloth a few minutes and rinse in cold water

SCARLET

Dip the cloth in a solution of alkaline or metalic salt, then in a cochineal dye, and let it remain sometime, and it will come out permanently colored. Another method is to take half a pound of madder, half an ounce cream tartar, one ounce marine acid, to a pound of cloth. Put it all together and bring the dye to a scalding heat. Put in your materials and they will be colored in ten minutes. The dye must be only scalding hot. Rinse your goods in cold water as soon as they come from the dye.

TO COLOR A BRIGHT MADDER

For one pound of yarn or cloth, take three ounces of madder, three ounces of alum, one ounce of cream tartar. Prepare a brass kettle with two gallons of water, bring the liquor to a steady heat. Then add your alum and tartar and bring it to a boil. Put in your cloth and boil it two hours, take it out and rinse it in cold water. Empty your kettle and fill it with as much water as before, then add your madder, rub it in fine in the water before your cloth is in. When your dye is as warm as you can bear your hand in, then put in your cloth, and let it lie one hour, and keep a steady heat; keep it in motion constantly, then bring it to a boil fifteen minutes, then air and rinse it. If your goods are new, use four ounces of madder to a pound.

DIFFERENT MODES OF DYING BLACK

Rub a brass kettle with soft soap, turn it upside down in a warm place twenty-four hours, then fill with soft water, rubbing the verdigris from the kettle into the water. Put your logwood in a bag and soak in a warm place several hours. Put your cloth in wet, and boil gently two hours or more, airing constantly and stirring well. Wash thoroughly before dyeing.

MORE BLACK

Soak your logwood chips in warm soft water one day to extract the strength, take out the chips and put in your goods, and soak them until well saturated with dye, stirring and turning often through the day. Then take out your goods and air them. Put an ounce of copperas in the dye, and when dissolved, dip your materials, raising and turning often a few minutes. Then take them out, air, and dry. Then wash in suds and sweet milk thoroughly and rinse, and you will have a fine black.

EVEN MORE BLACK

Logwood and cider, or vinegar, in iron, makes a good black for woolens.

Black inkpowder boiled in vinegar and set with a small bit of copperas makes a good black.

MAKING SOAP, ETC.

Soap cannot be made unless the lye is of the right strength, it must not be too weak nor too strong. And it sometimes occurs that when the lye is of the right strength that it will not form soap; the reason is that from exposure to atmospheric air it is deprived of a property essential to success. This may be remedied by lime. After boiling it with suitable proportions of grease and lye, and not being successful, put in a lump of lime, if not enough put in more and it will form soap, when every hope of success had fled.

Lye should be just strong enough to bear an egg; as large a spot as a shilling piece if it sinks below, or is borne up halfway it, will not do. Use three pounds of grease to a pail full of lye, and when it boils thick, it is ready to put away. Potash will make soap if dissolved by boiling, but it is not as good as hard wood ashes, put up in barrels or leaches for lye. To make a barrel of soap it will require five or six bushels of ashes; with four quarts of stone lime, if slacked, double the quantity. The lime should not be put at the bottom of the leach, but dissolved in two or three pails of boiling water, and turned on the ashes, after it has run a pail full or two of strong lye.

The barrel should have holes bored in the bottom and raised with four bricks, or a barrel without a bottom will do, with sticks and straw to keep the ashes in place, standing on a wide board with a channel cut for the lye to run. Soak the ashes by putting up a little water at a time a day or two, and then a gallon every hour or two, until the strength is exhausted.

VALUABLE RECEIPT FOR COLL SOAP

Cleanse your grease by putting in a little strong lye and boiling it thoroughly, then fill up with cold water, and the grease will float. Skim it off, melt it, put it in your barrel, and place it in the sun. Try the lye to have it the right strength, and heat it. Put in two pounds of grease to a pail full of lye and stir it every day. If it does not begin to look like soap in five or six days, add a little hot lye; if this does not help it, add grease. This mode some prefer. If made of potash, take twenty-five pounds of clean grease melted, eighteen pounds of potash, and dissolve in four pails of water; boil until dissolved. Put the grease and two pails of hot lye in a barrel, the next day another, and the next day another. Then fill up the barrel with hot water, a pail each day, stirring it well, and it will be nice soap. The sediment of the potash bad.

HARD SOAP

Dissolve twenty-five pounds of white potash in three pails of water. Heat twenty pounds of strained grease and add the lye and boil together until thick. Take it from the fire, stand in cold water until it becomes thin. Then put to each pail of soap a pint of salt and stir it well. Let it cool, and when hard take it from the lye and heat it over a slow fire. If you wish it to be a yellow color, put in a little palm oil and turn it in wooden vessels. When cold separate it again from the lye, cut it in bars, and let them stand in the sun several days to dry.

MORE HARD SOAP

Take eight pounds of soft soap; if you wish it nice, use that made of olive oil. Boil it two hours with six pounds of common salt and it will make five pounds of hard soap. Add a little rosin when you melt it over, and if you wish it nice, scent it with fragrant oil.

WINDSOR AND CASTILE SOAP

Slice the best white soap as thin as possible and melt it over a slow fire. Take it from the fire, and when lukewarm add oil of carraway enough to scent it, or other fragrant oil. Turn into molds and let it remain in a dry place five or six days.

Castile soap is made by boiling common soft soap in lamp oil three hours and a half.

NICE SHAVING SOAP

Take a quarter of a pound of Castile soap, one cake of old Windsor soap, a gill of lavender water, the same of Cologne water, and a little alcohol. Boil all these together until thoroughly mixed.

BAYBERRY AND MYRTLE SOAP

Dissolve two pounds and a quarter of white potash in five quarts of water. Mix, and boil over a slow fire, ten pounds of bayberry tallow or myrtle wax, till it turns into soap. Then add a teacup of cold water and boil ten minutes, scent with any fragrant oil, and turn in molds to dry. Let it stand in the molds a week or ten days and then remove it. This kind is good for shaving and chapped hands.

TO KEEP SOAP GREASE

It is often the case that no pains are taken to keep grease that is designed for soap away from flies and other insects, or from rats and mice. It may be kept clean and pure, so that the soap will be perfectly clean, by shutting it up in a box with a tight cover, or an iron pot with a close lid. It has been thus kept free of mold and other impurities through the heat of a long summer and is a great and essential improvement.

MISCELLANEOUS PRACTICALITIES

FOR INDELIBLE INK

To four drachms of lunar caustic in four ounces of water, add sixty drops of nutgalls made strong by being pulverized and steeped in soft water. The mordant, which is to be applied to the cloth before writing, is composed of one ounce of pearlash dissolved in four ounces of water, with a little gum Arabic dissolved in it. Wet the spot with this, dry, and iron the cloth, then write.

TO TAKE MILDEW OUT OF LINEN

Take soap and rub it well, then scrape on some fine chalk. Rub that also in the linen and lay it on the grass. As it dries wet it a little; it will come out at twice doing.

TO GIVE SILVER PLATE A LUSTER

Dissolve alum in strong lye, skim it carefully, then mix it with soap, and wash your silver using a linen rag.

FOR RED MARKING INK

Half an ounce of vermilion, one drachm of sal of steel finely levigated with linseed oil to a proper consistency.

RANCID OIL

May be restored to its original purity and sweetness by being heated with a certain quantity of calcined magnesia.

TO RESTORE THE COLOR OF WOOLEN CLOTH DISCHARGED BY AN ACID

Take equal parts of pearlash and quicklime dissolved in water and wet the parts with it. The place wet will become a reddish brown; a little vinegar now applied will restore it to its original black.

TO TAKE GREASE OUT OF SILK

Apply a little magnesia to the wrong side and the spots will soon disappear.

ANOTHER THAT NEVER FAILS, GOOD FOR CARPETS, WOOLEN, SILK, OR COTTON

Pulverize fine, new pipe stems or pipes, lay it on the spot, put a brown paper when you can under the cloth and one over the powder; set on it a warm iron, and it will extract all the grease if it remains sufficiently long.

TO MAKE COURT PLASTER

Dissolve isinglass, suspend your silk on a wooden frame by tacks, apply the glue with a brush, and let it dry; repeat it, and when dry cover it with a strong tincture of balsam of Peru. This is the real English court plaster, it is pliable and never breaks. The more common is covered over with the white of egg and dried.

TO MAKE A SIMPLE WHITE PAINT

Skim milk two quarts, fresh slack lime eight ounces, oil six ounces, white burgundy pitch two ounces, Spanish white three pounds. The lime to be slacked in water, exposed to the air, mixed in about one fourth of the milk the oil, in which the pitch is to be previously dissolved to be added a little at a time. Then the rest of the milk, and afterward the Spanish white. This quantity will cover twenty-seven yards two coats, and the expense not more than ten pence.

A CHEAP WATERPROOF PASTE

Take any kind of oil or lard, and mix with it India rubber cut fine, let it simmer over a slow fire until well incorporated, adding oil or lard until it is of proper consistency.

TO KEEP LEMON JUICE

Buy the fruit when cheap, roll them in the hand to make them mellow. Squeeze the juice into a china or earthen bowl, and strain it, not permitting the pulp to pass. Have ready ounce and half ounce vials perfectly dry. Fill them with the juice so near the top as to admit only half a teaspoonful of sweet oil into each, a little more in larger ones. Cork them and place them where it is cool. When you want it for use, take such a sized bottle as you will use in two or three days. Wind some clean cotton round a skewer, or a bit of wire, and just dip it in, the oil will all be absorbed, and the juice as fine as when first bottled.

TO MAKE COLOGNE WATER

Take a pint of alcohol, and put in thirty drops of oil of lemon, thirty of bergamot, and half a gill of water. If you desire musk, or lavender, add the same quantity of each. The oils should be put in the alcohol and shook well, before the water is added. Bottle it for use.

SIMPLE LIQUID BLACKING

Ivory black two ounces, sweet oil half a tablespoonful, brown sugar half an ounce. Mix them well and then gradually add half a pint of small beer, and a teaspoonful of gum Arabic. As it dissolves, shake it well and it is ready for use.

MAKE A VARNISH FOR CRAYONS, PENCIL DRAWINGS, ETC.

A thin wash of isinglass or gum Arabic put on with care will prevent them rubbing out. The same effect it is said may be produced by skimmed milk. It must be perfectly free from cream. Lay the drawing flat upon the surface of the paper, and take it up by one corner until it drains and dries.

INK POWDER FOR IMMEDIATE USE

Reduce to powder ten ounces of gall nuts, three ounces of green copperas, two ounces each of powdered alum and gum Arabic. Put a little of this mixture into white wine and it will be fit for immediate use.

TO PREVENT INK FROM FREEZING

Instead of water use brandy with the same ingredients that you use for any ink and it will never freeze.

TO PREVENT MOULD IN INKS

A quarter of a pint of spirits of wine may be added. The most simple and most effectual is to infuse a piece of salt as big as a hazel nut in each quart.

TO PREVENT TEAKETTLES COATING WITH LIME

Put the shell of an oyster in the teakettle and the lime will adhere to it, instead of coating the sides.

"WHITE WASH OF THE PRESIDENT'S HOUSE IMPROVED"

Take half a bushel of unslacked lime, and slack it with boiling water, cover it during the process. Strain it and add a peck of salt dissolved in warm water, three pounds of ground rice boiled to a thin paste put in boiling hot, half a pound of Spanish whiting, and a pound of clear glue dissolved in warm water. Mix and let it stand several days. Keep it in a kettle, and put on as hot as possible with a brush. It is said to look as well, and last as long, as oil paint on wood, brick, or stone. The expense is so trifling that great improvements should be the result.

A SIMPLE WHITEWASH

Slack as above, and add to each pail two double handsful of salt. Some think it an addition to add a double handful of fine sand, or sifted ashes, to make it thick like cream for the first coat. It covers smoke much better. This is better to be used hot. Coloring matter may be used if desired.

HOW TO HAVE A SHARP RAZOR

Take a strap of thick leather, such as is used for harness, and fasten at each end upon a piece of wood. Then rub upon its surface a piece of tin until it is smooth. It is said to be worth all the patent straps that have ever been invented.

PAINTING HOUSES

Repeated experiments prove that paint applied between November and March will last twice as long as that applied in warm weather. The reason is that in cold weather the component parts of the paint form a hard substance on the surface, as hard almost as glass, but in warm weather the oil penetrates the boards, and the paint soon wears off.

MULBERRY LEAF PAPER

Paper has been made of mulberry leaves, and has been used for writing and printing. It is said to be smooth, strong, and delicate, and may be either white or colored.

PREPARING QUILLS, BETTER THAN THOSE OF HAMBURG

Suspend in a boiler bunches of quills, fill with water just to touch their nibs. Close it steam tight, boil the water four hours, and take them out. The next day cut the nibs and draw out the pith, and rub them with a piece of cloth and expose them to a moderate heat. The following day they will have the hardness of bone, without being brittle, and be as transparent as glass.

TO MAKE INK FOR MARKING LINEN WITH TYPE

Dissolve one part of asphaltum in four parts of oil of turpentine, add lampblack or black lead in fine powder in sufficient quantity to render of proper consistence to print with type.

TO MAKE PATENT CEMENT

Lime, clay, and oxide of iron, separately calcined and reduced to a fine powder, are to be intimately mixed. Keep it close, and when used mix with a little water. It will make cracks in wood water-tight, etc.

CEMENT FOR STOVE PIPES

Cracks in stoves and pipes may be closed by a paste made of salt, ashes, and water. Iron filings, sal ammonia, and water make a harder and more durable cement.

SOAP FOR PLANTS

This is excellent for asparagus and peas, and for plants in pots it gives them a fine deep healthy green and makes them strong and luxuriant.

TO PREVENT DANGER FROM ICE

You can keep pavements and step stones clear of ice by sprinkling coarse salt on the ice. It will cause it to crack and thaw, and can be easily removed or swept away

ICE VAULTS IN CELLARS

Select a suitable place, and dig a hole five or six feet square and nearly as deep. Wall it with brick or stone. It may be improved by a double cover filled with tan bark, or tan laid over the ice six inches deep, and then a common cover.

REMOVING PUTTY

Moisten the putty with nitric or muriatic acid, and it may be removed at once. Strong soap will answer the same purpose.

CEMENTING GLASS OR CHINA

Provide some very finely powdered quick lime in a muslin bag. Take the broken ware and rub the edges with the beaten white of an egg. Take the lime and sift it thick over the edge rubbed with egg, press and bind the pieces together, and let them remain several weeks. For coarser crockery, rub the parts with white paint, made of white lead and linseed oil, press and bind until fully dry. They will last as long as new.

LABOR-SAVING SOAP

Take two pounds of sal soda, two pounds of yellow bar soap and ten quarts of water. Cut the soap in thin slices, and boil together two hours; strain and it will be fit for use. Put the clothes in to soak the night before you wash, and to every pail of water in which you boil them, add a pound of soap. They will need no rubbing, merely rinse them out, and they will be perfectly clean and white.

A FIRE PROOF GLUE OR CEMENT

Mix and boil together quicklime and linseed oil. It should be as thick as soft putty, and then spread on tin plates to dry hard. This when used should be melted like common glue and used while hot.

SIMPLE AND EAST METHOD TO EXTRACT GREASE

If the spot is small and light, simply laying magnesia on both sides, and warming it at the fire will do, by repeating. But if larger set on a warm iron. The pipe stems are surer for a large spot.

BLUE INK SPOTS

Blue ink should be first washed in sweet milk; then rub strong soft soap on the spot and it will soon disappear.

STAGGERS IN SWINE

Before giving anything, pour soft oil on the issues of their legs, and rub them well, then give as much new rum and pepper as you can make them take with a spoon. This it is said has cured those that were nearly dead. Nothing should be lost in giving something heating within.

TO TEMTPER NEW OVENS AND IRON WARE

Before new evens are used, they should be heated half a day and then put up the lid to keep the heat in. When heated the second time, they may be used for baking. If not treated in this way they will never retain heat well.

New flat-irons should be heated half a day before they are used. Iron ware of all kinds and stoves should be heated gradually at first or they may crack. Cold water if poured on hot iron will crack it.

TO REMOVE GREASE FROM BOARDS

Moisten clay or ground water lime with warm water, and after scraping the spot with a knife, lay it on and let it remain all night. If necessary repeat the process. This will soon remove it all.

TO CLEAN PAINT THAT IS NOT VARNISHED

Take a flannel and squeeze nearly dry out of warm water, and dip in a little whiting; apply to the paint and with a little rubbing it will instantly remove grease, smoke, or other soil. Wash with warm water and rub dry with a soft cloth. It will not injure the most delicate color, and makes it look as well as new; besides, it preserves the paint much longer than if cleaned with soap and water.

REMEDY FOR POISON

It is said that a gill of melted lard poured down the throat at of a sheep poisoned by eating laurel is a certain cure.

A DELICATE CEMENT FOR GLASS OR CHINA

One ounce of mastic and as much spirits of wine as will need to dissolve it. Soak an ounce of isinglass in water until quite soft, then dissolve it in rum or brandy until it forms a strong glue, to which add a quarter of an ounce of gum ammonia, well rubbed and mixed. Put the two mixtures together over a gentle heat until united, and keep in a vial well stopped. When used, place the vial in a kettle of warm water, warm the glass or china, and apply the cement, carefully fitting it together, keeping it close for twelve hours at least; it will then be sound, and the place scarcely perceptible.

TO TEMPER EARTHENWARE

When new, and before used for baking, put it in cold water to cover, and heat it gradually until the water boils. It is less likely to crack.

FOR MAKING BLACK INK

Take four ounces galls, two ounces copperas, one ounce of gum Arabic. Beat the galls and put them in a quart of warm soft water. Soak eight or nine days in the hot sun, or by the fire, shaking it often. Then add the copperas and gum, and it is fit for use in two or three days. The gum arabic must be dissolved in warm water, and a half ounce of alum powdered, added to the whole.

RED INK

Boil over a slow fire four ounces of Brazil wood chips in a quart of water till a third is evaporated; add while boiling two drachms of alum in powder. When the ink is cold, strain it through fine cloth. Vinegar may be used instead of water.

TO MAKE BLACKING

Put one gallon of vinegar into a stone jug, and one pound of ivory black well pulverized, a half pound of loaf sugar, a half ounce of oil of vitriol, and six ounces of sweet oil; incorporate the whole by stirring. This blacking is in great repute in different countries. It is less injurious than most blackings and produces a fine polish never to be surpassed.

TO RENDER CLOTH WIND- AND RAINPROOF

Boil two pounds of turpentine, and one pound of litharge in powder, and two or three pints of linseed oil. The article is to be brushed over and dried in the sun.

WHITEWASH THAT WILL NOT RUB OFF

Mix up half a pail full of lime and water, take half a pint of flour and make a starch of it, and pour it into the whitewash while hot. Stir it well and it is ready for use.

TO PREVENT IRON FROM RUSTING

Warm it and rub it with beeswax, put it to the fire until it has soaked in the wax, then rub it with a cloth. Or take fresh grease and rub, soaking it in by the fire.

TO PREVENT MOLDING IN BOOKS, INK, PASTE, AND LEATHER

Collectors of books will not be sorry to learn that a few drops of oil of lavender will insure their libraries from this pest. A single drop of the same will prevent a pint of ink from moldiness for any length of time. Paste may be kept from mold entirely by this addition, and leather is also effectively secured from injury by the same agency.

FIRE- AND WATERPROOF CEMENT

To a half a pint of milk, put an equal quantity of vinegar to curdle it. Take only the whey, and mix four or five eggs, beating the whole together. When mixed, add sifted quicklime until it acquires the consistence of a thick paste. With this, broken vessels and cracks of all kinds may be mended. It dries quickly, and resists the action of water, and a considerable degree of fire.

VARNISH FOR SHOES IMPERVIOUS TO WATER

Take a pint of linseed oil, six ounces of beeswax, two ounces of resin, half an ounce of mutton tallow, and melt them together, stirring them well. When about milk warm, apply it. The leather should be dry. Repeat it a few times warming it in, and no water can pass through, and it greatly increases the durability of boots and shoes.

TO CLEAN GOLD

Wash it in warm suds with ten or fifteen drops of sal volatile.

FIREPROOF CEMENT

Take as much lime as is usual in making a pot full of whitewash, and let it be mixed in a pail full of water; in this put two and a half pounds of brown sugar and three pounds of fine salt. If one pound of alum be added it will greatly improve the cement. Mix it well and it is completed. A little lampblack, yellow ochre, or other coloring to change the appearance, may be introduced. It is used as a protection against fire, and is considered valuable. The French use it to preserve the roof and to protect it.

GERMAN SILVER

Few are aware of the poisonous qualities of this compound. It is good for a variety of uses, but should never be used for spoons or vessels for cooking. It is composed of copper, arsenic, and nickel. It is oxydized by acids, and acts in the stomach as a slow but sure poison.

TO CLEAN KID GLOVES

White kid gloves may be kept nice by rubbing them when they are soiled, with India rubber. If it becomes necessary to wash kid gloves, take a piece of flannel, moisten it with a little milk, rub it on a cake of nice hard soap, and apply it to the soiled part of the glove. As soon as the dirt is removed, rub the spot with a dry piece of flannel. It should be done on the hand.

TO MAKE RED SEALING WAX

Take two parts of well-powdered shellac and one part each of resin and vermilion, mix them well together, and melt them over a gentle fire. When the ingredients seem thoroughly incorporated, work the wax into sticks. When shellac cannot be procured seedlac may be substituted. The resin should be of the whitest kind. Less vermilion may answer. If black is preferred, substitute ivory black. If green, use powdered verdigris, or any other color may be used.

TO REVIVE FADED BLACK CLOTHES

Boil two or three ounces of logwood in vinegar, and when the color is extracted, drop in a piece of carbonate of iron, which is of the same nature as rust of iron, as large as a chestnut; let it boil. Have the coat or pantaloons well sponged with soap and hot water, laying them on a table and brushing the nap down with a sponge. Then take the dye upon the table and sponge them all over with the dye, taking care to keep them smooth and to brush downward. When completely wet with dye, dissolve a large teaspoon of saleratus in warm water, and sponge all over with this, and it sets the color so completely that nothing rubs off. They must not be wrung or wrinkled, but carefully hung up to drain. The brownest cloth may be made a perfect black in this simple manner.

TO CLEAN A COAT OR PANTALOONS

Take brown hard soap and rub the collar where it is soiled well, and wherever there is a spot of oil, also the cuffs, and lower part of the sleeve. Have soft water boiling hot, dip out a pint, and lay the cuff and lower part of the sleeve in the scalding water until it acts upon the soap and soil, then take it out, and with a knife or the nail, take off the loose dirt, then dip again, and rub downward with the sponge, also cleaning inside of the cuff well. Then get another pint of hot water, and do the other in the same way. Then the collar which will need more hot water. When all the most soiled places are scalded and sponged, then soap a little water, do the coat all over, rubbing downward, then rinse in the same way with warm water, and finish off with the sponge wrung as dry as possible. Then hang up so as to preserve the shape, and drain and dry. This process will give to soiled clothes a luster, and an appearance of new cloth, besides making them perfectly clean. Pantaloons done in the same manner.

TO BLEACH WOOL, SILK, AND STRAW

Take a barrel, or box, and nail in muslin or gauze around the upper part, in a way to have it hang a little loose. If straw, first soak them well in pearlash water until they are golden yellow, then lay them in loosely over the muslin. When a little drained, take live coals into a kettle, or chaffing-dish, and sprinkle over some pounded brimstone, and set under the straw in the box or barrel; have it covered close at the top. Repeat this until they are bleached white; they should be stirred and made to lie as loose as possible whenever the fire is renewed. Silk and wool will bleach without being wet. The box or barrel should be open at the bottom, that the fire may be easily put under by simply raising it at one side. If bonnets, straw, or leghorn are stained or soiled, before bleaching, they should be washed clean with soap and water, and the stains taken out with tartaric acid. This does not injure the braid, and will make old hats look very white.

TO TAKE OUT FRUIT SPOTS

Wet the stain without dipping, and hold the part over a lighted common brimstone match at a proper distance. The sulphurous gas soon causes the spots to disappear.

TO TAKE OUT WAX

Put on spirits of turpentine or sulphuric ether. The marks of white paint also, may be discharged in the same way. Holding a red hot iron near to melt will sometimes answer by evaporation.

AN IMPROVED BLACKING

Take of ivory black and treacle, each twelve ounces; spermaceti oil, four ounces; white wine vinegar, four pints; mix. This not containing vitriol will not injure the leather.

STOPPING A LEAK

Take yellow soap and beat it up thick with whiting, and rub it into the leak; it will be found to stop it when other things have failed.

A CHEAP AND VALUABLE COMPOSITION FOR THE ROOFS OF HOUSES

Take one measure of fine sand, two measures of wood ashes sifted, three of slackened lime ground up with oil, laid on with a painter's brush, first coat thin and the second thick. It adheres strongly, and resists the action of fire.

REMEDY AGAINST FROST

Deposit wet strawy compost in the forks of a fruit tree when in blossom to protect the fruit from frost. If applied in the evening, and frost should occur in the night, it is said that it will be visible on its surface, but the fruit buds, or blossoms will escape injury.

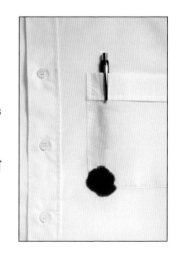

TO REMOVE INK FROM LINEN

Take pure tallow, melt it, and dip the spotted part into the tallow. Put it in the wash, and it will become perfectly white.

CURE FOR A WEN

Take alum salt, make a strong brine, simmer it on a fire, in which wet a piece of cloth and apply it for thirty successive days, and it will disappear.

SEWING ON GLAZED CLOTH

Pass a cake of white soap over any stiffened material, and the needle will penetrate with perfect facility.

BEEF

1. Sirloin. 2. Rump.
3. Edge bone. 4.
Buttock. 5. Mouse
buttock. 6. Leg. 7. Thick
flank. 8. Veiny piece. 9.
Thin flank. 10. Fore rib:
seven ribs. 11. Middle
rib: four ribs. 12.
Chuck rib: two ribs. 13.
Brisket. 14. Shoulder,
or leg of mutton piece. 15 Clod. 16. Neck, or sticking piece. 17. Shin.
18. Cheek.

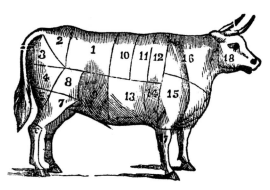

MUTTON

1. Leg. 2. Shoulder. 3. Loin,
best end. 4. Loin, chump end.
5. Neck, best end. 6. Breast. 7.
Neck, scrag end.

Note.—A chine is two loins:
and a saddle is two loins and two
necks of the best end.

MUTTON.

PORK.

1. Leg. 2. Hind loin. 3. Fore loin.
4. Spare rib. 5. Hand. 6. Belly or
spring.

PORK.